# THE INVASION
# 1941

*It will be the duty of the Air Force to paralyse and eliminate the effectiveness of the Russian Air Force as far as possible. It will also support the main operations of the Army, i.e. those of the central Army Group and of the vital flank of the Southern Army Group. Russian railways will either be destroyed or, in accordance with operational requirements, captured at their most important points (river crossings) by the bold employment of parachute and airborne troops.*

*In order that we may concentrate all our strength against the enemy Air Force and for the immediate support of land operations, the Russian armaments industry will not be attacked during the main operations. Such attacks will be made only after the conclusion of mobile warfare, and they will be concentrated first on the Urals area.*

*Adolf Hitler*
*Extract from Directive No. 21, Operation 'Barbarossa'*
*18 December 1940*

GW01390060

# June-December 1941

## Operation Barbarossa

When Adolf Hitler launched Operation 'Barbarossa'[1], his attack against the Soviet Union, he took the first steps towards achieving what he regarded as two of his life's main goals: the destruction of the "cradle of Communism" and the creation of *Lebensraum*; living space in the East for the German people.

Preparations for the launching of 'Barbarossa' were immense. Assembled against the Soviet Union's western frontiers were 3.6 million German and other Axis soldiers, 600,000 vehicles, 3,600 tanks and more than 3,000 first-line aircraft, the total might of which formed the largest invasion force the world had ever seen. When the invasion began, *Reichsmarschall* Hermann Göring's *Luftwaffe* was undoubtedly the most effective air force in the world. Combining modern aircraft with new tactics and a high standard of aircrew training, Germany's air force was without parallel and the Spanish Civil War, the *Blitzkrieg*, and the Battle of Britain had created a core of immensely experienced airmen. In the fighter force, the Bf 109 F-4, the latest version of *Professor* Willy Messerschmitt's single-engined fighter, was without peer.

Opposing the German forces, the Red Army was numerically superior but had been debilitated by Josef Stalin's autocratic rule. On the day of the German invasion, the Soviet Union possessed a total of approximately 20,000 combat aircraft, including 11,500 fighters, but the vast majority of these aircraft, especially the vulnerable twin-engined SB bomber, the I-153 biplane fighters and the slow Polikarpov I-16 *Ishak* (known to the Germans as the *Rata*), were technically inferior[2]. Although in June 1941 a new generation of Soviet fighter types was about to enter service with first-line units, only the Yak-1 could compete on relatively equal terms with the Bf 109 E or F-2, while the MiG-3 and the LaGG-3 were both slower and less manoeuvrable. In addition, most Soviet aircraft had no radio transmitters installed, whereas this was standard equipment in all *Luftwaffe* aircraft and was a key instrument in the *Jagdwaffe's* air combat tactics.

New Bf 109 Fs, Professor Messerschmitt's outstanding fighter aircraft, in this instance belonging to 3./JG 51, photographed at Mannheim in early 1941. The aircraft in the background is coded 'Brown 3' and neither machine has yet received any unit emblems.

However, the technical inferiority of Soviet aircraft in mid-1941 should not be exaggerated as the situation was more a question of high proficiency on the part of the Germans than low Soviet standards. Indeed, the performance of the majority of Soviet-designed aircraft in 1941 was generally higher than in most other air forces and the Il-2 *Shturmovik,* just beginning to reach front-line units in June 1941, was probably the best ground-attack aircraft anywhere. Far worse for the Soviet armed forces was that they still suffered from the effects of Stalin's Great Purge of 1937/38 when the intelligentsia and tens of thousands of officers were liquidated. In the wake of these persecutions, the Soviet government decided to shorten pilot training with the result that thousands of newly trained pilots, barely able to take off and land their aircraft, were forced to meet the best airmen in the world. Moreover, 91 per cent of all commanders of larger Soviet Air Force units had held their posts for less than six months.

The Soviet airmen were further impaired by outmoded tactics. As in all but the German and Finnish air forces, they continued to fly in outdated, inflexible three-aircraft V-formations, and their general doctrine was defensive rather than offensive. Furthermore, they were frequently instructed to patrol a specific territorial area and were not allowed to pursue even damaged enemy aircraft beyond the borders of that area. Later, many *Luftwaffe* crews on the Eastern Front were saved due to this practise, which also resulted in the proportion of repairable *Luftwaffe* aircraft being higher on the Eastern Front in 1941 than anywhere else. In contrast, the pilots of the *Jagdwaffe* were encouraged to fly

1. Named after a medieval crusader.
2. The Germans erroneously referred to the SB as the Martin bomber, SB-2 or SB-3, while the I-153 *Chayka* was frequently misidentified by the Germans as a Curtiss.

aggressively and experience during the Battle of Britain had shown that the best way to protect bombers was not to keep the fighters in slow-flying close escort missions, but to employ them in *freie Jagd* missions in which they hunted for potential opposition in the target area.

On 21 June 1941, the air forces of the Soviet Army and Navy, collectively known as the VVS (*Voyenno-Vozdushnye Sily,* Military Air Force), had less than half the country's total number of combat aircraft stationed in the western regions. The Army Air Forces in the western regions were divided into five military districts which, after the German attack, were reformed into Army Groups, or Fronts, as follows:

**VVS Northern Front** and **VVS North-Western Front**, both positioned along the Finnish border and in the Soviet-occupied Baltic states.

**VVS Western Front** positioned in the Soviet-occupied parts of Poland.

**VVS South-Western Front** in north-western Ukraine.

**VVS Southern Front** in south-western Ukraine.

In addition, there were the Naval Air Forces of the Northern Fleet in the Far North (VVS SF), the Red Banner Baltic Fleet (VVS KBF), the Black Sea Fleet (VVS ChF) and the long-range (strategic) bombers, the DBA.

This Bf 109 F-2 coded 'Yellow 2', was flown by Lt. Erich Viebahn of 3./JG 51 and was photographed on 21 June 1941, the day before 'Barbarossa'. A few weeks later, on 13 July, Viebahn was severely wounded and although he did not return to Russia, he later flew with several Experten of JG 50.

I./JG 51 badge

**Messerschmitt Bf 109 F-2 'Yellow 2' flown by Lt. Erich Viebahn of 3./JG 51, June 1941**
**The camouflage on this aircraft is typical of the factory scheme in which the majority of Bf 109 F's were finished on the eve of Operation 'Barbarossa'. All undersurfaces are Light Blue 76, with the wings and fuselage upper surfaces in a splinter pattern of 74 and 75, with the fuselage mottles of 74 and 75 being enhanced with 02 and Green 70. However, once the campaign was under way, it became evident that this colour combination was not entirely suitable for use in all conditions and many units began to introduce their own modified schemes, the most frequently seen being a change to a dark green, more suitable for use over the forested areas of Russia.**

# June-December 1941

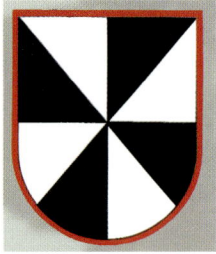

II./JG 3 badge

*RIGHT*: This Bf 109 F-2 coded 'Yellow 1' was photographed at Monchy Breton in France in May 1941. It was flown by Oblt. Heinrich Sannemann, the Staffelkapitän of 6./JG 3, and is shown here with an all-yellow engine cowling shortly before the unit transferred to the East. Prior to 'Barbarossa', Oblt. Sannemann, who led 6./JG 3 from 23 November 1940, claimed three victories, principally while with the Stab of II./JG 3 where, with Franz von Werra, he formed the "Max and Moritz" team (See Vol. 2 Section 3, Page 208.)

*BELOW LEFT AND RIGHT*: Two further photographs showing Sannemann's 'Yellow 1' at Mariupol on 12 July 1941, where it is seen after returning from a sortie in which his aircraft was hit by the defensive fire from a Russian bomber. Fortunately, the aircraft had been recently modified with an armoured windscreen, and this saved Sannemann's life. Note also that by this time the upper and side surfaces of the engine cowling had been camouflaged. Sannemann, who claimed his eleventh victory on 8 August, a few days before this incident, was thus more fortunate than his colleague Oblt. Karl Faust, Staffelkapitän of 4./JG 3 with 14 victories, who made an emergency landing at Chernyakhosk in enemy-held territory on 12 July and was shot by Russian soldiers.

## Messerschmitt Bf 109 F-2 'Yellow 1' flown by Oblt. Heinrich Sannemann, Staffelkapitän of 6./JG 3

The completely Green 70 spinner on this machine lacks the one-third white segment specified in Luftwaffe painting instructions, but this aircraft is otherwise typical of the appearance of Luftwaffe fighters immediately prior to 'Barbarossa' and during the opening months of that campaign. The camouflage scheme consists of the then standard 74/75/76 finish with the fuselage mottled in 02, 74 and 75. The yellow engine cowling is also typical of the period, although the Luftwaffe High Command would soon issue an order stating that only the undersurface of the cowling was to be yellow. The black area over the wing root was intended to hide exhaust staining and also to make it easier to clean off carbon deposits. Originally applied at unit level, this area tended to become larger and, particularly once the Fw 190 entered service, so highly stylised that it began to compromise the camouflage finish. Note that this aircraft was later fitted with an armoured windscreen.

# June-December 1941

## Deployment of major German and Soviet Air Commands on 22 June 1941

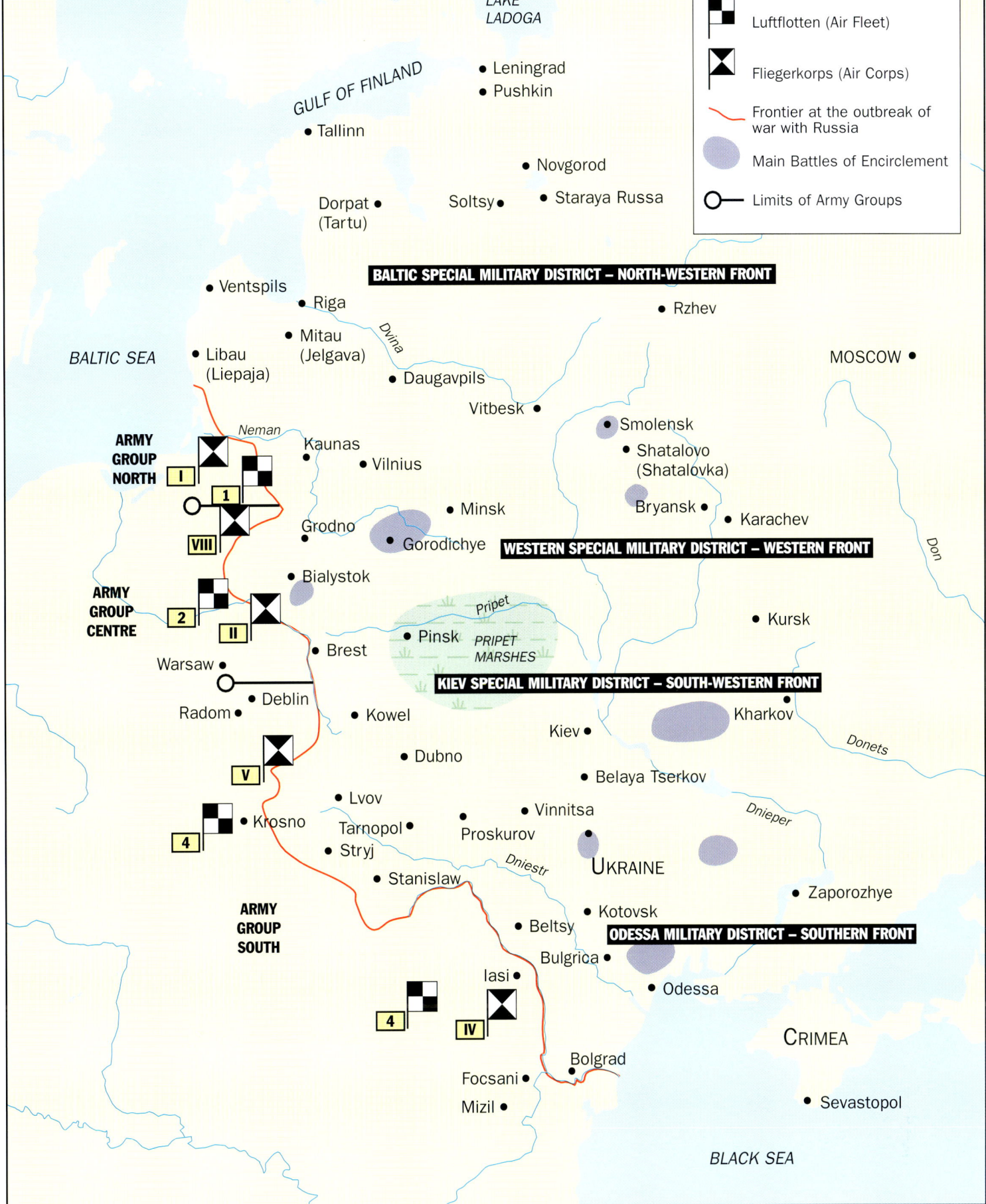

LAKE LADOGA

GULF OF FINLAND

• Leningrad
• Pushkin

• Tallinn

• Novgorod

Dorpat • (Tartu)

Soltsy •
• Staraya Russa

**KEY**

■ Luftflotten (Air Fleet)

✖ Fliegerkorps (Air Corps)

― Frontier at the outbreak of war with Russia

● Main Battles of Encirclement

○― Limits of Army Groups

**BALTIC SPECIAL MILITARY DISTRICT – NORTH-WESTERN FRONT**

• Ventspils

• Riga

• Mitau (Jelgava)

Dvina

• Rzhev

BALTIC SEA

• Libau (Liepaja)

• Daugavpils

MOSCOW •

Vitbesk •

Neman

• Smolensk

**ARMY GROUP NORTH**

Kaunas •

• Vilnius

• Shatalovo (Shatalovka)

**I**

**1**

• Minsk

• Bryansk

• Karachev

Grodno •

**VIII**

• Gorodichye

**WESTERN SPECIAL MILITARY DISTRICT – WESTERN FRONT**

• Bialystok

Pripet

**ARMY GROUP CENTRE**

**2**

**II**

• Pinsk

PRIPET MARSHES

• Kursk

• Brest

Warsaw ○

**KIEV SPECIAL MILITARY DISTRICT – SOUTH-WESTERN FRONT**

Radom •
• Deblin

• Kowel

Kiev •
• Kharkov

**V**

• Dubno

Donets

• Belaya Tserkov

• Lvov

• Vinnitsa

Dnieper

**4**

• Krosno

Tarnopol •

Proskurov •

Dniestr

• Stryj

UKRAINE

• Zaporozhye

• Stanislaw

**ARMY GROUP SOUTH**

• Kotovsk

• Beltsy

**ODESSA MILITARY DISTRICT – SOUTHERN FRONT**

Bulgrica •

• Odessa

Iasi •

CRIMEA

**4**

**IV**

• Bolgrad

Focsani •

Mizil •

• Sevastopol

BLACK SEA

June-December 1941

## "The Rata was a difficult opponent…"

WALTER STENGEL, 6./JG 51

On the eve of *Barbarossa*, the *Staffel's* kills, listed on our victory board, showed that I had only two victories. Our *Kommodore*, Werner Mölders, said that that would soon change… At 04.30 on 21 June 1941, I took off with my 6./JG 51 on our first mission against Russia. We still saw trains heading east and west across the Russian border but the airfields near the front were filled with Russian aircraft, which leads me to believe that the Russians were going to attack us. On this occasion, we had no encounter with enemy aircraft and landed nearly two hours later.

We had a quick breakfast while our machines were refuelled and re-armed and, as the whole of II./JG 51 had landed after the first sorties without any victories, when we took off again, we hoped for better luck. This time, at about 07.30 hrs, my 6. *Staffel* encountered a flight of enemy aircraft and myself and at least two other pilots each shot down a *Rata*, thus winning for II./JG 51 the first victories on the new front. We landed and as soon as possible took off again on another mission. This first day was typical of those that followed, though we often had to move in order to keep pace with the advance of the ground troops.

We found at first that the *Rata* was a difficult opponent to shoot down and a whole flight could attack one *Rata* without success. The problem was that we approached it too rapidly so there was too little time to shoot at it, but after about eight days, we knew what to do and kills on the Eastern Front became really easy. At this time, the required number of victories for the *"Dödel"* (*Ritterkreuz*) kept increasing and my fate was that once I had shot down the required amount, the number went up. When I scored 18 kills, the number required had increased to 20; when I had 20, 25 were required; when I had 25 kills, 30 were required, and so on.

We flew many low-level missions but the cost was out of proportion to what was achieved. In Russia, I was shot down three times, in each case making a crash-landing, always a great risk in unfamiliar territory, and on 18 occasions returned to base with hits in my aircraft. Because we flew at low level, the Russians fired at us with everything they had, whereas over England we had flown at such great altitudes that even the British heavy anti-aircraft guns did not bother us.

In December 1941 we retreated, and during the Winter of 1941/42 I was at Briansk where we were surrounded by partisans.

## 22 June 1941

Operation '*Barbarossa*' opened in the early hours of 22 June 1941 with massive *Luftwaffe* attacks against 31 major Soviet airfields from the Baltic Sea in the north to the shore of the Black Sea in the south. Not only were the Soviets caught totally by surprise, but the Soviet Army Air Forces in eastern Poland and the Baltic states were in the middle of a re-equipment programme which resulted in the airfields in the western parts of the USSR being completely overcrowded. Hundreds of aircraft were therefore destroyed in the first attack wave alone, during which the Bf 109s of the *Jagdgeschwadern* mainly carried out low-level attacks in which they strafed the rows of parked aircraft and dropped SD-2 bombs. Four Bf 109s led by the *Staffelkapitän* of 4./JG 27, *Oblt.* Gustav Rödel, managed to put no fewer than 45 Soviet aircraft out of commission with their SD-2s during a single raid and JG 51, commanded by *Obstlt.* Werner Mölders, claimed to have destroyed a total of 129 Soviet aircraft on the ground. Later, the fighters flew as escort for bomber and Stuka formations as well as flying *freie Jagd* sorties.

Weary German infantry take a short rest during the early days of the drive to the East.

The initial Soviet response to the German attack was sporadic and lacked any central co-ordination, but the first aerial encounters nevertheless revealed several surprises. Not only did the Soviets display a stiff determination to fight, but *Jagdwaffe* pilots were alarmed when the Polikarpov fighters they were pursuing suddenly made a snap 180-degree turn and counter-attacked head-on. Moreover, several German aircraft were brought down by deliberate air-to-air ramming, the so-called *tarans*, one early victim of this tactic being *Major* Wolfgang Schellmann, *Geschwaderkommodore* of JG 27, who was captured and shot by the NKVD.

Despite the destruction of hundreds of their aircraft on the ground, the Soviets immediately began sending waves of SB and DB-3 medium bombers against the invaders. In some cases,

# June-December 1941

*RIGHT*: Major Wolfgang Schellmann, the Kommodore of JG 27, seen far left, introduces his men to General von Richthofen, commanding officer of VIII. Fliegerkorps. Also seen are Hptm. Max Dobislav, Kommandeur of III./JG 27, and his Adjudant, Oblt. Kripenkohl.

*LEFT*: On 22 June, Major Wolfgang Schellmann, the Kommodore of JG 27 (shown here while still a Hauptmann) either collided with debris from his 26th victory, an I-16, or was rammed by an I-153. In either event he was forced to bale out of his Bf 109 E-7 which was marked with the double chevron of a Geschwader-kommodore and came down in Soviet-held territory. Although he tried to reach the German lines he was captured and, in all probability, shot two days later by the NKVD. Schellmann, who had received the Ritterkreuz on 18 September 1940 while Kommodore of JG 2, was posthumously promoted to Oberstleutnant. Coincidentally, he was succeeded as Kommodore by Major Bernhard Woldenga, whom Schellmann had earlier replaced in the Autumn of 1940.

*ABOVE*: Just as JG 27 lost a great ace on the first day of 'Barbarossa' when Major Wolfgang Schellmann was shot down, JG 53 also lost Hptm. Heinz "Pietzsch" Bretnütz, the Kommandeur of II./JG 53. On the eve of Barbarossa, Bretnütz - pictured here in the Spring of 1941 - had 32 victories not including those achieved in Spain. On 22 June, however, just after he shot down his 33rd victory, an SB, his aircraft was hit. His comrades saw him crash-land behind enemy lines but no more was heard of him until the 26th. Meanwhile, his pilots tried to devise a plan to rescue their extremely popular commanding officer but it was soon realised that this was unrealistic. In fact, he had already been found by a farmer, who hid him until German troops reached the area, but Bretnütz had been badly wounded in the legs and because of the delay in transferring him to hospital, his wounds had become gangrenous. An attempt to save his life by amputating his left leg failed and Bretnütz died on 27 June. He was buried in Insterburg on 1 July and was temporarily succeeded as Kommandeur by Hptm. Spies.

these bombers succeeded in inflicting severe casualties among German ground troops but, in the main, their efforts resulted only in a series of losses. Lacking radio equipment, the Soviet bombers flew in open echelon formations so that each pilot could remain in visual contact with the formation leader, even though this made concentrated defensive fire against *Luftwaffe* fighters impossible. In addition, due to the general chaos, almost all bomber missions had to be flown without fighter escort and scores of bombers were lost. Thus, while German bombers and Stukas continued to pound Soviet airfields, the Bf 109s attacked the relentless waves of Soviet bombers. These astonished the *Luftwaffe* fighter pilots with their tactics, for even when attacked the bomber pilots took no evasive action whatsoever but maintained their course, often until all were shot down. Such a fate met Soviet Bomber Regiment 39 BAP, which lost all 18 SBs despatched against German forces crossing the River Bug. Similarly, II./JG 53 shot down eight of 40 SBAP's SBs but, in this engagement, the *Gruppenkommandeur, Hptm.* Heinz Bretnütz, was obliged to make a forced landing in Soviet-controlled Lithuania. Badly injured and requiring urgent hospital treatment, Bretnütz was hidden by friendly locals until rescued four days later by advancing German troops. He was then taken for immediate medical treatment and although his left leg was amputated in an attempt to save his life, Bretnütz, a Knight's Cross holder credited with 37 aerial victories, died soon afterwards.

The repeated clashes between German fighters and Soviet bombers continued, and at about 09.30 hrs, 1./JG 51's *Lt.* Heinz Bär and his wingman, *Ofw.* Heinrich Höfemeier, were escorting a damaged He 111 back over German-controlled territory. In the Siedlce area, they spotted a formation of 25 to 30 SB bombers without any fighter escort. The two German pilots immediately attacked, at the same time calling for reinforcements. Höfemeier succeeded in shooting down four of the bombers, his first victories in the war, before he was forced to break off because of a bullet wound in his left arm. Bär shot down another two, his 19th and 20th victories, and when other JG 51 pilots arrived on the scene they destroyed six more SBs. JG 51's *Geschwaderkommodore, Obstlt.* Mölders, also claimed four victories which increased his total number of victories to 72 [3].

Without doubt, the *Luftwaffe* played a key role during the onslaught on 22 June and, had it not been for its successful actions, the VVS would have inflicted severe blows against the German forces. On 22 June, the Germans claimed to have destroyed 1,489 Soviet aircraft on the ground and 322 in the air. According to Soviet figures, more than 800 aircraft were destroyed on the ground and 336 were shot down in the air. These figures underline the vast technological and tactical superiority enjoyed by the *Luftwaffe*, quite apart from its superior training and combat experience. Conversely, the stiff Soviet resistance can be seen in *Luftwaffe* losses in the East on 22 June, which were by no means light: 111 aircraft lost [4] due to enemy action on this day alone, including 61 totally destroyed or written off.

3. This figure does not include victories in Spain.
4. A loss indicates the number of machines lost to front-line service due to enemy action. Thus, in this instance, of the 111 aircraft lost to front-line service, 61 were totally destroyed or otherwise written off.

# June-December 1941

# "We all feel that a powerful drama is unfolding..."

HANNES TRAUTLOFT, JG 54

I arrive at the airfield at 02:30 while stars still shine in the dark skies. As a result of the cool night, dew covers the clover underfoot and my fur-lined flying boots are damp. The airfield is alive with activity. In the parking places, 45 engines are being warmed-up and create a monotonous roar as the chief mechanics rev them up. Bright, blue-yellow flames shoot from the exhaust stubs and the air is filled with a rare scent from the mixture of soil, flowers, grass, petrol and oil. As the eastern skies are tinged with colour, there is the first chirping of birds and the shadows and darkness quickly disappear. Everyone on the airfield is aware that this is the dawn of a fateful day.

Shivering, we climb into our aircraft. The metal seat is cold and the harness is damp. The chief mechanic straps me in and wishes me luck as I close the canopy. The engine starts with a thunder. As always before a combat mission, my throat is dry and perhaps my heart is beating faster than normally. At 02.50 hrs we take off. The order is for all *Geschwader* of the I. *Fliegerkorps* to cross the border at 03.00 and as we fly over it, the front comes alive. At 03.05, heavy artillery is brought into action and everywhere, all along the front, we see the muzzle flashes of the guns. It is a rousing scene, and at this moment the Eastern Front is born. From our vantage point we can see to the north across the Memel River, while to the south the Romintener Heath is visible. We all feel that a powerful drama is unfolding, that a door is being opened on a new phase of history, but one which will possibly be fateful for us all.

We fly in the direction of Kowno. The pilots fly nervously. I recognize this from the first operations of previous campaigns. It is due to anxiety, as so much is unknown: What will the Russians do? Will our surprise attack succeed? Will the Russian fighters engage in combat? Are their aircraft superior to ours? Before and below us on the dark ground is the city and airfield of Kowno, which can be identified only through its outline and contours. At this moment the sun rises above the eastern horizon, suddenly bringing glittering rays of light on our aircraft as we fly through the crystal-clear air of the dawn of a new day.

Our bombers attack the airfield at Kowno, the bombs landing in the middle of the parked aircraft. Suddenly, there are two fighters in front of us, but they disappear as quickly as they had appeared. There is no combat with them. We fly back. Numerous fires blaze along the entire front and thick black columns of smoke rise high in the sky.

The Russians were not prepared in any way for the first, surprise attack and most of their bases are attacked without any resistance. Soon, however, this situation changes and our bases at Gerlinden and Lindental report that they have spotted enemy bombers flying overhead. The alert squadrons take off to prevent the penetration of East Prussian airspace and, of the 26 SB 2 bombers which enter the area, 17 are shot down. Everywhere we see parachutes and burning, crashing aircraft. The other enemy aircraft flee in a wild panic but are followed all the way to Schaulen. We fly operations throughout the day, each pilot flying five to seven sorties. Our spines and backs ache. Escort for bombers, fighter sweeps, and low-level attacks are alternated. This afternoon we gained air superiority over our area. No Russian fighter dares to appear.

During a fighter sweep late that afternoon, we carry out a surprise attack on an enemy bomber formation which consists of 50-60 SB 2s. Unfortunately, because we are short of fuel we can only make two attacks. The first one is unsuccessful, but during the second, the right engine of the bomber in front of us is burning. The aircraft jettisons its bomb load but then explodes in the air. As we turn away, we encounter strong return fire from the tail gunners in the other bombers. The enemy formation flies south, but our fuel shortage compels us to return to base. We radio for reinforcements which intercept this formation and shoot down another 11 aircraft. One of our Me 109s has been hit and is unable to lower its landing gear. The pilot makes a careful and successful crash-landing. One hour later we take off for our next mission. One pilot loses his bearings during air combat but reports from Litzmannstadt in the late afternoon.

Toward dusk we fly one last mission in the direction of Schaulen but there is no contact with the enemy. We fly low over our ground troops who are half way to Kowno and Schaulen. Dense clouds of dust reveal the direction of the advance of each column, just as in Poland. There are fires everywhere; entire villages are in flames. Tauroggen is burning and produces a large column of black smoke which can be seen from far away. After the final mission, the successes of the day are reported to the *Fliegerkorps*. The *Geschwader* destroyed 45 aircraft in the air and 35 on the ground.

The strain of the day's fighting is very noticeable. We are all dog-tired and need rest, but this is a bad time for fighter pilots to sleep and we are unable to relax until the middle of the night. After just two hours, however, we have to prepare for the next day's operations.

During the first days of the invasion the Luftwaffe destroyed many Soviet aircraft on the ground.

# June-December 1941

*RIGHT*: The wrecks of various Polikarpov I-16s which fell into German hands when their airfield was captured. The scene shown was recorded on an airfield used by JG 51.

*BELOW AND BELOW RIGHT*: JG 54 was based on this airfield where, in addition to the camouflaged I-16, there was also a parked Yak-1.

*LEFT*: This wreck of the dive-bomber version of the twin-engined Tupolev SB was discovered on a Russian airfield used by II./JG 54. In the background is a Bf 109 F-2, 'White 6', of 4./JG 54.

# June-December 1941

Officers of 7./JG 54 photographed at Schlossberg, near Insterburg, on 22 June 1941. From left to right: Lt. Peter-Ferdinand von Malapert-Neuville, Lt. Helmut Biederbick, Lt. Max-Hellmuth Ostermann and (possibly) Lt. Leister.

## The Fight for Air Superiority

After 22 June 1941, *Luftflotten* 1 and 2 continued attacking Soviet airfields, reportedly destroying another 1,357 Soviet aircraft on 23 and 24 June. Meanwhile, devastating strikes were flown against Soviet troop positions, marching columns and headquarters in the rear area. The German 2., 3. and 4. *Panzergruppen* charged through Soviet defence positions which were in increasing disorder and surrounded large parts of Soviet Army Group Western Front. In view of the weak aerial opposition by the VVS in this sector on 23 June, *Luftflotte* 2's fighter units were able to carry out low-level attacks against airfields and retreating Soviet columns.

To the north, *Luftflotte* 1's fighter units, JG 54 and 4. and 5./JG 53, were in action against VVS Baltic Military District which had suffered heavily from the first day's attack but was still able to maintain continuous air activity throughout 23 June, on which date is was redesignated VVS North-Western Front. Before dawn on 23 June, ten Soviet bombers raided the East Prussian city of Königsberg and at 10.00 hrs, 16 SBs were despatched against Gumbinnen aerodrome in East Prussia. They were intercepted by *Stab* and II./JG 54, and not a single Soviet aircraft returned to its base. Less than two hours later, nine 7./JG 54 pilots commanded by 9./JG 54's *Staffelkapitän, Oblt.* Hans-Ekkehard Bob, bounced ten SBs to the north of Kaunas. All ten SBs were shot down, two of them by *Lt.* Max-Hellmuth Ostermann. The last SB, piloted by the Soviet formation leader, was shot down by *Oblt.* Bob, but in the process, Bob's own Bf 109 was hit by the bomber's defensive fire. He forced-landed in Soviet-controlled territory but returned to the German lines two days later.

In total, JG 54 claimed 39 victories on the second day of 'Barbarossa' but, owing to the confused situation, German fighter pilots frequently attacked their own bombers by mistake and at least five of the Ju 88s lost by KG 76 and KG 77 on 23 June were shot down by friendly fighters. During the late afternoon a Ju 88 returned fire, shooting down and killing 5./JG 54's *Uffz.* Walter Puregger.

With new reinforcements arriving, VVS Western Front was able to increase its activity on 24 June. Its fighters, mainly from fighter division 43 IAD, which had been spared the destruction of 22 June, were assigned to air defence tasks in the Minsk region. Here, six I-16s from 43 IAD's fighter regiment 163 IAP, led by *St.Lt. (Starshiy Leytenant,* Senior Lieutenant) Zakhar Plotnikov, fell upon 27 Ju 87s from II. and III./St.G. 1 and shot down six within a matter of minutes. Meanwhile, the *Jagdgruppen* were fully occupied dealing with the re-appearing Soviet bombers from both the DBA and VVS Western Front. These flew without any fighter escort and attacked the advancing German *Panzer* columns. On one occasion, III./JG 27's Bf 109 E pilots observed 27 DB-3s from Long-Range Bomber Regiment 53 DBAP which were intent on attacking advance elements of 4. *Panzergruppe.* III./JG 27 claimed seven of the bombers shot down in this engagement, while 53 DBAP's records show that in fact nine were lost, eight of them to Bf 109s. There were similar scenes over the advance columns of 2. *Panzergruppe* advancing further to the south, where *Oblt.* Karl-Heinz Schnell, *Staffelkapitän* of 9./JG 51, destroyed seven SBs, four of them in only four minutes, while *Lt.* Ottmar Maurer of the same *Gruppe* shot down another six. JG 51's score for the day was 57 victories, all against SB bombers.

On 25 June, as the Soviet Western Front collapsed in the face of Army Group Centre's armoured spearheads, *General der Flieger* Wolfram *Freiherr* von Richthofen brought forward many units of VIII. *Fliegerkorps* in order to render air support, including *Stab,* II. and III./JG 27 and III./JG 53, which moved up to the large aerodrome at Vilnius which had been captured on the 24th. As soon as Soviet aerial reconnaissance established that the Germans were using Vilnius aerodrome, all available bombers were despatched to neutralise the Germans on the ground. In fierce air fighting against repeated attacks by formations each of ten to 20 SBs and DB-3s throughout the day, the Bf 109 pilots at Vilnius claimed 54 Soviet bombers shot down for the loss of a single Bf 109. *Stab* and III./JG 53 claimed 30 of these kills, including four by JG 53's *Geschwaderkommodore, Major* Günther *Freiherr* von Maltzahn, while II./JG 27 contributed 24, seven of them by *Lt.* Gustav Langanke, which brought his total claims to eight. To the south, JG 51 brought down another 68 SBs, six of them by *Oblt.* Hans Kolbow. These few examples illustrate perfectly the Soviets' determination and also how helpless were the SBs against intercepting German fighters. Nevertheless, the German victories were not easily achieved, and every interception was met by frantic defensive fire from the bombers' gunners who were equipped with extremely rapid-firing machine-guns. Frequently it was reported that Soviet gunners refused to bale out of their stricken machines and kept firing at the Bf 109s until their aircraft crashed. However, only a few Bf 109s were totally destroyed in air combat although many others were severely damaged as, for example, in JG 51, where a total of 18 Bf 109s were put out of commission on 24 and 25 June.

Because of insufficient deliveries of spare parts, an increasing number of the German combat aircraft were grounded, often as a result of only minor damage or technical faults which could not be rectified due a lack of spare parts. After a week of fighting in the East, the number of serviceable German aircraft in *Luftflotten* 1, 2 and 4 had dropped from 1,939 to 960. Nor was German fighter production significantly increased, but built up only slowly from an average of 156 machines per month during the second half of 1941 to only 243 during the first half of 1941, after which production actually dropped below even this relatively low level. These facts indicate that not only were German preparations for Operation 'Barbarossa' insufficient, but also that they had not properly prepared for war on more than one front.

The situation, however, was infinitely worse for the Soviets. On 26 June, Soviet long-range bomber division 40 DBAD, to which 53 DBAP belonged, was unable to carry out any operations. On the same day, other DBA units recorded 43 DB-3s lost in efforts to halt the invaders. When 2. and 3. *Panzergruppen* completed their pincer movement at Minsk and surrounded approximately 400,000 troops of the Soviet Western Front, the VVS in the area had virtually bled to death. In their desperation, the Soviet commanders brought together their last reserves and, on 30 June, launched them against the German Berezina River bridgehead at Bobruysk. First the Soviet aircraft ran into the concentrated fire from the *Luftwaffe's Flakregiment* 10. The dispersed bombers were then attacked by the Bf 109s of JG 51 which within six minutes also completely annihilated another group of 22 Soviet bombers that attempted to attack one of JG 51's airfields. Thus, when the day was over, JG 51 had claimed 113 victories against five combat losses. The *Geschwaderkommodore, Obstlt.* Werner Mölders, as well as *Hptm.* Hermann-Friedrich Joppien and *Lt.* Heinz Bär, each scored five victories, bringing Mölders' total score to 82 and Joppien's to 52. With this, JG 51's victory tally surpassed the 1,000 mark, about 400 of which had been attained since 22 June 1941.

Mölders and General Guderian in discussion at the end of June or beginning of July 1941. Standing between them is Hptm. Hermann-Friedrich Joppien, who had become Kommandeur of I./JG 51 on 18 October 1940.

# June-December 1941

Similar scenes occurred in the skies over Army Group North on the last day of June, when the Soviets made fruitless attempts to prevent 4. *Panzergruppe* from crossing the Daugava River at Daugavpils. The DBA and Army bomber forces in this area had been so weakened that VVS KBF, the Red Banner Baltic Fleet, had to be called in for this task. Approaching without fighter escort at altitudes of up to 7,000 feet, the DB-3s and SBs of bomber brigade 8 BAB were attacked by JG 54 which claimed to have shot down 65 bombers before they could fulfil their task but in fact destroyed 43. JG 54's losses amounted to five Bf 109s and two pilots.

According to Soviet figures, 1,669 Soviet aircraft were lost in the air alone between 22 and 30 June 1941 so that on 1 July, VVS Western Front could muster no more than 500 aircraft. In view of the weakening Soviet resistance in the air over the German Centre Front, the *Luftwaffe* could afford to re-allocate its units and while parts of VIII. *Fliegerkorps* were transferred north to support the drive by 4. *Panzergruppe* towards Leningrad, II./JG 27 left the Eastern Front entirely and moved to the Mediterranean area of operations.

While the VVS adopted more defensive tactics, concentrating on fighter interception or strafing missions in daylight and bombing at night, the huge salients between Bialystok and Minsk were compressed. Up to 9 July, Army Group Centre took more than 300,000 Soviet troops as prisoners and captured 3,332 tanks and 1,809 artillery pieces. By that time, too, the Germans estimated, probably without exaggeration, total Soviet aircraft losses to be 6,223, of which 1,900 had been shot down in aerial combat.

Under the terms of the 1929 Geneva Convention, troops from the combatant nations who fell into the hands of an opponent were guaranteed several basic rights including humane treatment and restrictions on the duties they could be forced to perform. The USSR, however, was not a signatory to the Convention and surrender or capture did not therefore guarantee the lives of Red Amy soldiers. Before 'Barbarossa', Hitler instructed his Wehrmacht leaders that the campaign would be a war of annihilation and that they were to dissociate themselves from any idea of soldierly comradeship. As a result of the German Army's subsequent cruel and callous treatment of an estimated 5.7 million Russian PoWs, it is believed that no less than one in three, i.e. over three million, died from thirst, hunger, exposure, disease, brutal treatment and overwork. Even after their return home at the end on the war, large numbers of the PoW survivors were, on Stalin's orders, either executed or imprisoned for the 'crime' of being captured or contaminated by anti-Soviet ideals. This scene of Russian prisoners being forced to assist in the construction of a bridge in the fierce Summer heat, was photographed in July 1941. Needless to say, few if any of these men would have survived.

# June-December 1941

*BELOW*: This Bf 109 E, 'White 2' of 7./JG 27, seen on a Russian airfield during the opening stages of 'Barbarossa', has just performed a "Kopfstand", or "Headstand", more frequently referred to as a "Fliegerdenkmal", or "Pilot's Monument". Note that traces of the Stammkennzeichen, ending in the letters 'PG', may still be seen on the side of the fuselage.

*ABOVE RIGHT*: Although the loss rate for JG 27 was relatively light during the opening stages of 'Barbarossa', Fw. Friedrich Grimpe (shown here as an Unteroffizier in France) was killed in action on 28 July 1941, 7. Staffel's second fatality. On the day he died, Grimpe had shot down his third victim.

*ABOVE AND LEFT*: This badly damaged Bf 109 E, 'White 3' of 7./JG 27, was normally flown by Lt. Rolf Seitz and was photographed on 1 August 1941. Presumably, to judge from the damage, the aircraft was destroyed as a result of a Soviet bombing attack. Note that the uppersurfaces have been camouflaged in a non-standard, two-tone finish as seen on the tail section laying on the wing.

# June-December 1941

*ABOVE*: Oblt. Karl-Gottfried Nordmann of IV./JG 51 returning after a mission. This Gruppe was formed in February 1941 from I./JG 77 and, changing its silver shoe emblem to a black one on a shield, retained it as its own.

*RIGHT*: Bf 109 F-2 'Brown 5' of 12./JG 51 after a landing accident early in the Russian campaign. The fuselage shows signs of extensive repainting and the machine-gun troughs on the engine cowling have been painted red, or black. This aircraft is probably one of the four Bf 109 Fs of IV./G 51 which were damaged in landing accidents at Prusana on 24 June 1941, a fifth aircraft being similarly damaged at Krezewica on the same day. Later, this Staffel was led by Oblt. Heinz Bär, who took command on 20 July 1941 after his predecessor, Oblt. Karl-Gottfried Nordmann, replaced Major i.G Beckh as Kommandeur of IV./JG 51.

*LEFT*: Hptm. Josef Fözö was appointed Kommandeur of II./JG 51 on 21 February 1941 and, by the time 'Barbarossa' began, already had 15 victories in the West plus another three from his time in Spain. On 11 July 1941, Fözö claimed his 24th victory but was severely wounded when his Bf 109 F-2, W.Nr. 12836, crashed at Stara-Bychow. After recovering from his injuries, he returned to the front in May 1942 as Kommandeur of I./JG 51.

*LEFT*: Heinz Schumann flew in Spain with the Legion Condor and claimed five victories during the Battle of Britain and another one in early 1941. In Russia he flew with I./JG 51 and became very successful, claiming another 12 victories between 21 June and the end of July. In this view, Oblt. Schumann is pictured with a Bf 109 F fighter-bomber loaded with four 50 kg bombs on a centreline ETC. Later, in December 1942, Schumann became Staffelkapitän of 10.(Jabo)/JG 2 which operated with considerable success against shipping in the English Channel and in carefully planned raids against coastal targets in Southern England.

*BELOW LEFT*: This Bf 109 F was flown by Eichenlaubträger Hptm. Hermann-Friedrich Joppien, the Kommandeur of I./JG 51. Before his death on 25 August 1941, Hptm. Joppien (*BELOW*), seen here wearing the Oak Leaves, was credited with 70 victories, although there are no victory bars marked on this aircraft.

**Messerschmitt Bf 109 F flown by Hptm. Hermann-Friedrich Joppien, Kommandeur of I./JG 51**
Lacking victory bars or even a unit emblem, the overall appearance of this aircraft, although carrying the fuselage markings of a Gruppenkommandeur, provides no indication that it was flown by one of the most important of the Luftwaffe's fighter pilots. Camouflage is the standard 74/75/76 scheme with mottles of 02, 74 and 75 on the fuselage.

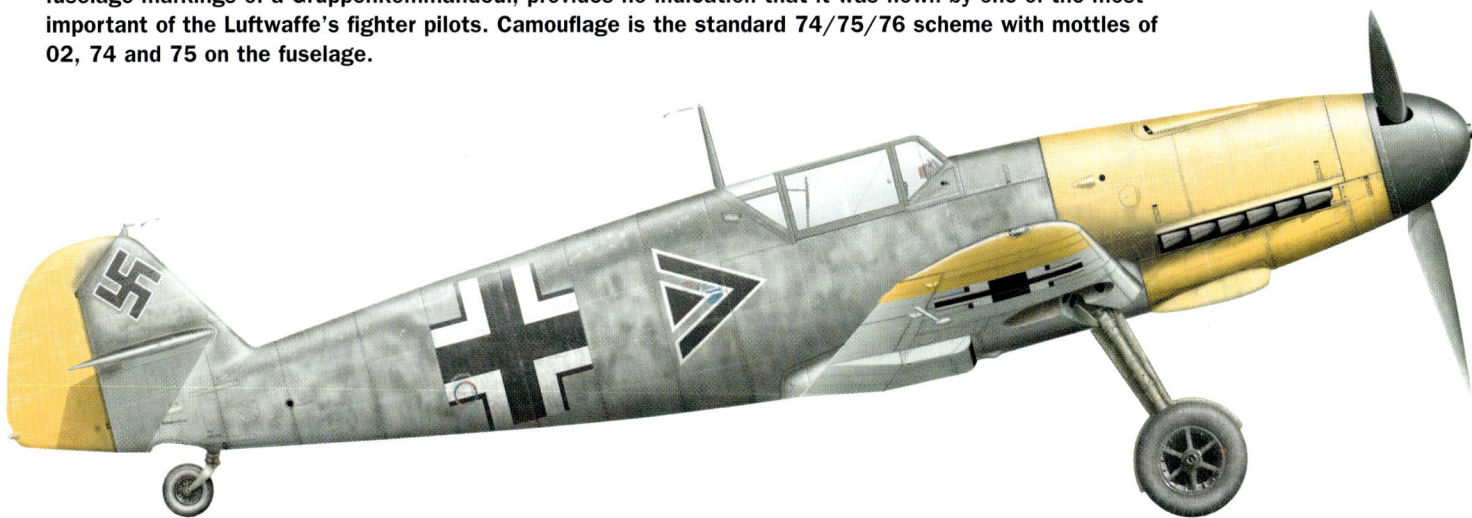

## The Advance Through the Baltic States

By 30 June 1941, VVS North-Western Front, responsible for air cover in the Baltic states, had lost almost 900 aircraft to enemy activity, including 425 lost in the air. In addition, VVS KBF had been dealt a heavy blow during its failed attempt to halt the German advance at the Daugava River in south-east Latvia. With air support reinforced by parts of VIII. *Fliegerkorps*, 4. *Panzergruppe* swarmed across the Daugava on 2 July and continued its advance to the north-west. VVS Northern Front, the only Soviet air fleet in the western territories to escape the devastation of the first days of the war, was immediately brought forward to help counter this threat. Between 4 and 6 July, following a brief lull caused by adverse weather, VVS Northern Front carried out a series of large-scale operations against 4. *Panzergruppe* but failed even to slow the German advance. Instead, in these three days, the Russian formations were met by fully alerted German fighter units which claimed 121 victories, most being destroyed over Latvia by *Hptm.* Dietrich Hrabak's II./JG 54 which, on 5 July, exceeded its 300th victory. On the Soviet side, VVS Northern Front's composite air divisions 2 SAD and 41 SAD alone registered 60 combat losses during operations against German advance columns between 4 and 9 July.

As the SB and DB-3 bombers started to disappear due to their enormous losses, so larger numbers of fighters from VVS Northern Front and VVS KBF started confronting the German fighters and Soviet opposition grew stronger. Thus, when 7./JG 54's *Lt.* Max-Hellmuth Ostermann claimed his 19th and 20th victories on 6 July, he saw two of his fellow pilots shot down while three I-16 pilots of 154 IAP claimed to have shot down three Bf 109s without loss to themselves. On 7 July, 11 of JG 54's Bf 109s were destroyed or severely damaged, and six of the *Geschwader's* best pilots, all from III./JG 54 and including the *Gruppenkommandeur*, *Hptm.* Arnold Lignitz, were posted missing as a result of missions on 6 and 7 July. On 6 July, *Oblt.* Heinz Lange had just shot down one of the VVS's new Pe-2 bombers when his Bf 109 F-2 'Black 5', W.Nr. 6781, was severely damaged and forced landed close to a German *Flak* battery. At the same time, *Lt.* Erwin Leykauf's Bf 109 F-2, 'Black 3', W.Nr. 6788, was damaged by a 202 SBAP SB's rear gunner over enemy-held territory and came down in marshland where Leykauf managed to evade detection. *Hptm.* Lignitz was the first of these pilots to return and immediately set out in a Bf 108 liaison aircraft to search for his missing comrades. He found Leykauf, stark naked, trying to dry his wet clothes. Much to the relief of *Major* Hannes Trautloft, *Geschwaderkommodore* of JG 54, it was later reported that the Bf 108 had returned to Ostrov aerodrome with another four of the six missing men.

Although I. *Fliegerkorps* reportedly shot down 487 Soviet aircraft and destroyed another 1,698 on the ground between 22 June and 13 July, the *Luftwaffe's* numerical superiority was in fact deteriorating. Indeed, on 9 July, *Hptm.* Dietrich Hrabak's II./JG 54 reported that only five of its 40 Bf 109s were serviceable and the strength of *Luftflotte* 1 was reduced to 350 aircraft. Facing *Luftflotte* 1 were some 1,300 [5] Soviet aircraft comprising most of the combined forces of VVS North-Western Front, VVS Northern Front and VVS KBF.

By mid-July, German Army Group North had driven the Soviets from Lithuania and Latvia and was advancing into Estonia and towards Leningrad in Russia itself, but the German motorised units had been severely depleted and their supply lines stretched. On 14 July, the Soviet 11th Army counter-attacked 4. *Panzergruppe* at Soltsy, west of Lake Ilmen. The powerful Soviet strike was supported by an *ad hoc* force of 235 aircraft commanded by *General-Mayor* Aleksandr Novikov, the new commander of the united air forces of the former North-Western and Northern fronts, now known as VVS Northern District. The German *Panzer* troops were thrown back, parts of 8. *Panzerdivision* were surrounded, and a *Staffel* of II./JG 54 was forced to abandon the advanced airfield at Porkhov. Meanwhile, other German airfields in the area were subjected to small but surprisingly effective raids by modern Pe-2 bombers. In one such attack at Pskov, a single Pe-2 caused a number of casualties and injured several of II./JG 53's personnel.

Even though 8. *Panzerdivision* was eventually saved, it was clear that the *Blitzkrieg* in the north had ended. Even more apparent, especially to the ground troops of Army Group North, strafed relentlessly from mid-July 1941 by Soviet fighter-bombers, was that the VVS was far from defeated.

Between 22 June and 19 July 1941, the *Luftwaffe* recorded 774 of its own aircraft destroyed (including 216 fighters) and 510 (including 187 fighters) severely damaged on the Eastern Front.

*Hptm. Dietrich Hrabak climbing from the cockpit of a MiG-3. The pilot standing looking at the red star marking is Ritterkreuzträger Oblt. Hans Philipp, the Staffelkapitän of 4./JG 54.*

---

5. Includes a few hundred aircraft based along the Soviet–Finnish border.

June-December 1941

Photographed at Sebesaya, Bf 109 F-2 'Yellow 4' (*BELOW*) was flown on 12 July by the Staffelkapitän of 6./JG 54, Lt. Hans Beisswenger (*RIGHT*) when he claimed his 18th victory. Remarkably, Beisswenger had claimed his first victory just three months earlier when, during the war in the Balkans, he shot down a Yugoslav Hurricane on 7 April. He received the Ritterkreuz on 9 May 1942, when his total stood at 47 victories, and received the Oak Leaves before he was posted missing on 26 September 1942 after claiming a total of 152 victories.

**II./JG 54 badge**

### Messerschmitt Bf 109 F-2 'Yellow 4' flown by Lt. Hans Beisswenger, Staffelkapitän of 6./JG 54, July 1941

The II./JG 54 first began to experiment with this form of camouflage during the latter stages of the Battle of Britain and it remained in use throughout the early stages of the Russian campaign. Here, the fuselage top decking and spine are finished in two greys, either mixed or early examples of 74 and 75, with the Pale Blue 76 fuselage sides covered in patches of 02, around which are sprayed meandering lines of Green 70. On this machine, one half of the Green 70 spinner has been painted white and the tip is yellow. Eighteen victory bars appear on the rudder.

# June-December 1941

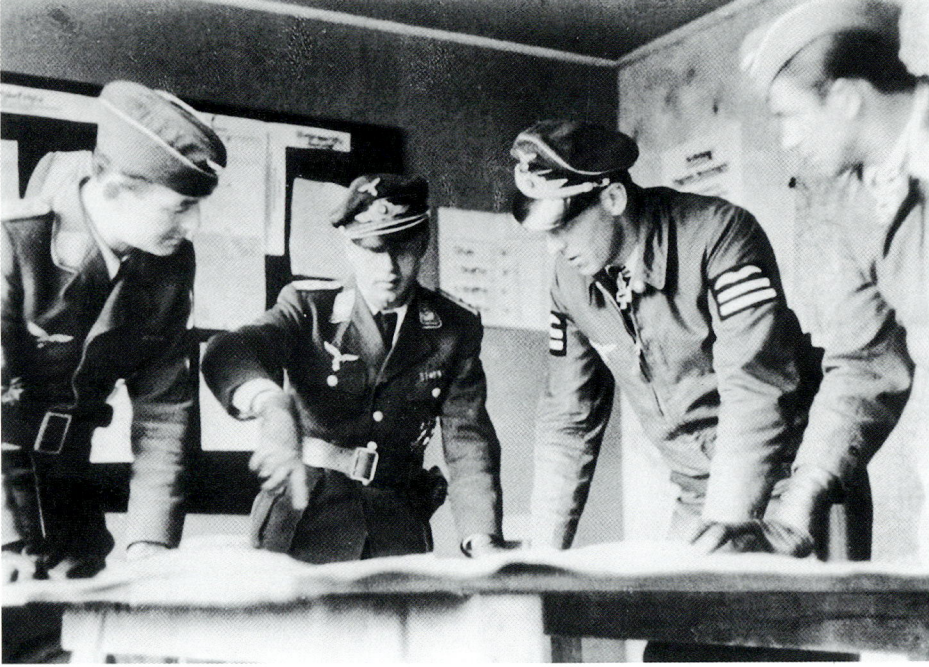

*BELOW*: On 13 July 1941, Oblt. Gerhard Ludwig of Stab I./JG 54 hit an obstacle and was killed when his aircraft crashed. Like many other German pilots of the Second World War, he received only a primitive grave.

*ABOVE*: Officers of JG 54. From left: Oblt. Reinhard Seiler, who returned as Staffelkapitän of 1./JG 54 on 28 June 1941 after having recovered from wounds suffered on 5 August 1940; Hptm. Dietrich Hrabak, Major Hannes Trautloft and Oblt. Hans Philipp.

*BELOW*: A Bf 109 F-2, believed to have been flown by the Gruppenadjutant of II./JG 54, on a Russian airfield. The horizontal bar of II. Gruppe is barely visible on the rear fuselage but the 'Lion of Aspern' emblem just in front of the windscreen is obscured by the tree trunk in the centre of the photograph.

# June-December 1941

*THIS PAGE*: This Bf 109 F was another of the aircraft flown by Hptm. Dietrich Hrabak, the Kommandeur of II./JG 54. Hrabak (*RIGHT*) claimed 16 victories in the West and by 30 July had increased his score to 24. For the rest of the year his duties as Kommandeur restricted his operational flying but, in 1942, he again flew many operations and added further to his tally.

# June-December 1941

## Into the Ukraine

*BELOW*: At the start of 'Barbarossa', Major Günther Lützow, since 21 August 1940 the Kommodore of JG 3, had already been credited with 18 victories and had been awarded the Ritterkreuz on 18 September 1940. On 20 July 1941, Lützow received the Oak Leaves in recognition of his 40th victory but, on the same day, he had already increased his score by claiming his 41st and 42nd victories. Here, Lützow is seen (left) with his Adjutant, Oblt. Rudolf von Mentzingen, who had claimed his second victory on 1 August but who was later killed near Novaya Greblya, approximately 50 km NW of Kiev, on 10 August.

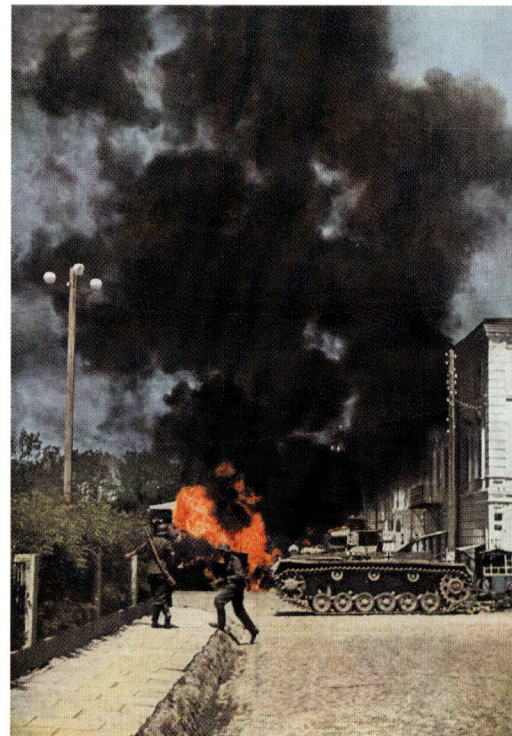

As in the north, it was important that the *Wehrmacht* should destroy Soviet forces before they could withdraw into the interior. However, Army Group Centre, which was to advance in the direction of Moscow, was separated from Army Group South, which was to advance into the Ukraine, by the Pripet Marshes, a huge natural barrier running in an east-west direction through eastern Poland. Furthermore, Army Group South was split geographically from *Luftflotte* 4 by neutral Hungary. From its positions in southern Poland, 1. P*anzergruppe*, supported by V. *Fliegerkorps,* attacked south of the Pripet Marshes and advanced towards the city of Kiev. Further south, the German 11th Army and Rumanian forces remained waiting along the Rumanian–Soviet border. These forces were supported by IV. *Fliegerkorps*, the fighter component of which consisted of *Stab,* II. and III./JG 77, plus I.(*J*)/LG 2 and certain Rumanian fighter units.

As in the north, VVS units opposing Army Group South and *Luftflotte* 4 were very active during the first days of the invasion. This was particularly the case in south-eastern Poland, where VVS South-Western Front (formerly VVS Kiev Special Military District) and DBA units went into action against the advancing German *Panzer* spearheads. The main task of *Major* Günther Lützow's JG 3, the *Jagdgeschwader* available to V. *Fliegerkorps*, was to clear the skies of Soviet aircraft through *freie Jagd* missions over the advancing *Panzer* columns and, on 23 June, this unit claimed 38 victories, mostly SB and DB-3 bombers. The offensive operations by V. *Fliegerkorps'* bomber units operating in support of the ground troops had to be carried out mainly without fighter escort, but few Soviet fighters were encountered in the air and German losses were very limited. To the south, *Stab,* II. and III./JG 77 and I.(*J*)/LG 2 carried out bomber escort missions and also flew *freie Jagd* and ground-strafing sorties against airfields, claiming 16 victories on 23 June against a single combat loss.

The most effective Soviet resistance in the air during the early days of 'Barbarossa' was that which met *Luftflotte* 4, and on 24 June Soviet bombers succeeded in inflicting severe losses on 1. *Panzergruppe* while II./JG 3 claimed only three victories but lost two of its own pilots. Over Bessarabia, II./JG 77's *Fw.* Otto Köhler was killed, possibly shot down by St.Lt. Aleksandr Pokryshkin of Fighter Regiment 55.

In Rumania, the task of III./JG 52, part of the *Deutsche Luftwaffenmission Rumänien,* was to protect the Rumanian oilfields. This units had recently exchanged its old Bf 109 Es for the latest Bf 109 F-4 which was fitted with the powerful 1,350 hp DB 601N engine and armed with the very effective MG 151/20 automatic cannon. As a result of the *Gruppe's* defensive duties, it did not participate in operations over the frontline for several weeks, but on 24 June, 36 Soviet bombers of the Soviet Black Sea Fleet attacked the Rumanian oilfields and airfield at Constanta. In their first attack, the Soviet aircraft succeeded in returning without loss, but when the bombers attempted a second raid later that day, III./JG 52 was scrambled to intercept and the Bf 109 F-4s shot down a total of 32 SBs and DB-3s, ten being destroyed in the first few minutes. It was during this engagement that *Uffz.* Gerhard Köppen of 7./JG 52, later to become one of the *Gruppe's* top scorers, achieved his first victory.

By this time, V. *Fliegerkorps* had been reinforced by the arrival of I.(*J*)/LG 2 and *Stab* and I./JG 53, and for the next few days these units and the original JG 3 flew

*ABOVE*: South of the Pripet Marshes, Feldmarschall von Runstedt's Army Group South met stiff Soviet opposition before reaching Zhitomir but then advanced and surrounded Uman.

*BELOW*: Two pilots of III./JG 77 at Iasi in July 1941 with, in the background, a Bf 109 F-4 coded 'White 8' of 7. Staffel.

# June-December 1941

in defence of the airspace over 1. *Panzergruppe*. On 25 June, the Soviet bomber crews flew a total of 780 sorties against 1. *Panzergruppe* in the Brody area, claiming the destruction of 30 tanks, 60 other vehicles and 16 artillery pieces, but the bombers were unprotected and so many formations of SBs and DB-3s were destroyed that soon there was almost none left. During these attacks, a *Schwarm* from II./JG 77 led by *Oblt*. Walter Hoeckner reportedly destroyed ten out of a force of 12 SBs, eight being claimed by Hoeckner alone. On 25 and 26 June, hundreds of Soviet aircraft were destroyed and by 30 June, the fighter units of *Luftflotte* 4 had claimed approximately 380 victories. German combat losses in this period were just 15, but the level of serviceability was steadily declining and in II./JG 3, for example, after one week of war in the East, the number of serviceable Bf 109s had been reduced from 32 to 20.

One of the most skilful *Jagdwaffe* pilots serving with *Luftflotte* 4 during this period was *Hptm*. Walter Oesau, *Gruppenkommandeur* of III./JG 3. Already a holder of the Knight's Cross and Oak Leaves awarded during the Battle of Britain, Oesau increased his victory tally from 42 to 50 between 22 and 30 June 1941, and on 1 July he destroyed three Soviet bombers, followed by another three on 6 July and four on the 8th. In Oesau's *Gruppe*, *Oblt*. Kurt Sochatzy, *Staffelkapitän* of 7./JG 3, also emerged as a successful pilot. Claiming only his second aerial victory on 26 June, by 9 July, on which date he shot down five Soviet bombers, he had increased his tally to 18.

Between 22 June and 5 July 1941, Soviet units opposed to *Luftflotte* 4 lost a total of 1,218 aircraft. However, they were soon replaced and from around 10 July, Soviet air activity against Army Group South started to mount. That day, two pilots of II./JG 3 spotted 12 TB-3s flying in formation without any fighter escort. The two Bf 109 pilots, *Oblt*. Franz Beyer and *Uffz*. Werner Lucas, attacked and claimed to have shot down five of the huge four-engined bombers although the records of the bomber unit in question, Heavy Bomber Regiment 14 TBAP, show that in fact seven were lost. Meanwhile, in

*BELOW AND RIGHT*: Oblt. Kurt Sochatzy, Staffelkapitän of 7./JG 3. An Austrian pilot, Sochatzy was absorbed into the Luftwaffe and later fought with the Legion Condor in Spain. In Russia, he was shot down on 16 July 1941 and although posted missing for several hours, returned to his unit. On 3 August 1941, by which time he had claimed 38 victories, his aircraft was deliberately rammed and Sochatzy became a prisoner. The photograph (*BELOW*) shows Sochatzy with his chief mechanic and his 'White 1' in France shortly before the Russian campaign. Painted under the cockpit is the name 'Tizi'.

# June-December 1941

III./JG 3, only six serviceable Bf 109 F-2s remained on 11 July, but these were flown by the best pilots including *Hptm.* Oesau, who achieved another five victories on 10 July, a further seven on the 12th and three days later received the Swords for 80 victories. On 15 July, 9./JG 3's *Ofw.* Hans Stechmann brought JG 3's victory total to over 1,000 by shooting down three I-153s.

In mid-July, the Soviets' situation in the Ukraine deteriorated considerably when, on the 16th, 1. *Panzergruppe* seized Biyala Tserkov, south-west of Kiev, and wheeled southwards towards Pervomaisk. The next day, the German and Rumanian armies in Rumania started their main offensive across the Dniestr River and advanced northwards to meet 1. *Panzergruppe* and encircle Soviet forces at Uman in a giant pincer movement. Since the entire railway system in the rear area had been destroyed by *Luftflotte* 4's bombers in one of history's most effective air interdiction operations, Soviet troops in the area were deprived both of supplies and much of their freedom to manoeuvre. Furthermore, the four weeks of air action against VVS forces in the area had been so effective, that in 282 sorties flown by JG 77 and I.(*J*)/LG 2 on 17 and 18 July in support of the drive from the south, they met virtually no Soviet opposition.

To the north, large parts of V. *Fliegerkorps* were concentrated on a huge airfield near Biyala Tserkov, from where operations to support the continued drives against both Uman and Kiev were flown. Biyala Tserkov was typical of the kind of airfield soon to become familiar to German forces on the Eastern Front, being virtually nothing but a huge, flat field where the personnel usually were billeted in tents.

*ABOVE:* Walter Oesau (right) with General Robert Ritter von Greim, commander of V. Fliegerkorps. Soon after this photograph was taken, Oesau was posted to command JG 2 in France.

*ABOVE AND RIGHT:* A view of Herbert Ihlefeld's Bf 109 E in Russia. It carries the emblem of I.(Jagd)/LG 2 under cockpit and 47 victory bars on the rudder. (*RIGHT*) A closer view of the victory record on Ihlefeld's rudder. The last victory bar, the 47th, is dated 12 July 1941.

June-December 1941

*LEFT AND BELOW*: The incredible number of victories claimed by the Jagdflieger in the Summer of 1941 undeniably resulted in a race to achieve the required total necessary to receive the Ritterkreuz. At the beginning of 'Barbarossa', several pilots received the award after 20 victories, but this number progressively increased to 25 and then 30. In this photograph (*LEFT*), Oblt. Robert Olejnik, since 17 May the Staffelkapitän of 1./JG 3, has already been awarded an imitation Ritterkreuz after claiming his 20th victory on 3 July 1941. (*BELOW*) To show the victory which gained him the Ritterkreuz, Olejnik's 20th Abschussbalken was painted on the rudder of his aircraft in white. Olejnik received a real Ritterkreuz by 6 July, on which date he also claimed his 21st victory, although in fact the official date of the award is 30 July, by which time he had increased his score to 32 victories, this total including five British aircraft during the Battle of Britain. On 14 August, Olejnik's Bf 109 F was hit in the radiator during combat with I-16s and although he had to make an emergency landing near Vassilikov, he was unhurt.

*BELOW*: On 1 July 1941, the day Hptm. Franz von Werra, the famous escaper, took over I./JG 53 from Oblt. Ignaz Prestele who temporally replaced Oblt. Wilfried Balfanz (KIA on 24/6/41). On 6 July, von Werra claimed his ninth victory, an SB-2. (For more information about Franz von Werra, see 'Battle of Britain' Section 3 pages 207 to 213.)

During this period, *Major* Günther Lützow's JG 3, operating on Army Group South's northern flank, played a particularly important role, being ordered to cover the north, where the German 6th Army was advancing eastwards towards Kiev, and also to support the drive in the south aimed at surrounding the Soviet troops at Uman. JG 3 carried out fighter sweeps over the area of the German advance and escorted the dive-bomber unit St.G. 77, which had been transferred from *Luftflotte* 2 to support Army Group South's battle of encirclement. During this time, *Major* Lützow achieved his 42nd victory on 20 July and was awarded the Oak Leaves. *Oblt.* Robert Olejnik, I./JG 3's most successful pilot, received the Knight's Cross on 30 July for 32 victories and three days later, *Oblt.* Viktor Bauer, *Staffelkapitän* of 9./JG 3, also received the Knight's Cross for 34 victories. Operating in the same area as JG 3 were *Stab* and I./JG 53, which had also been brought in from *Luftflotte* 2. JG 53's *Kommodore*, *Major* Günther *Freiherr* von Maltzahn, was awarded the Oak Leaves on 24 July when he claimed his 42nd victory. Meanwhile, one of the Luftwaffe's most famous pilots, the escaper *Hptm.* Franz von Werra, *Gruppenkommandeur* of I./JG 53, increased his victory total from eight to 21 in slightly more than three weeks. Owing much to the air support provided by such experienced pilots, the German armies linked up at Pervomaisk on 3 August and trapped the Soviet armies in the Uman area.

The effectiveness of the earlier *Luftwaffe* attacks on the Russian railway system now worked to the detriment of the German forces and resulted in severe supply difficulties. Aircraft serviceability in *Luftflotte* 4's units was badly affected and dropped rapidly during the second half of July so that by the 31st, I./JG 3 was down to only seven serviceable Bf 109s. At the same time, while the strength of the VVS Southern Front had dwindled from 671 aircraft on 1 July to 258 on 1 August, the surviving Soviet airmen nevertheless continued to put up a determined resistance. III./JG 3 was dealt a severe loss on 3 August, when

# June-December 1941

June-December 1941

*RIGHT*:
On 1 August 1941, III./JG 52 flew from Mizil in Rumania to Belaya-Tserkov in Russia, and at 04.40 hrs the next morning flew its first mission escorting Ju 87s. At this time, III./JG 52 was the only Gruppe in the Geschwader equipped with the Bf 109 F-4 and on its first day of operations two Bf 109 F-4/Bs were seriously damaged after running out of fuel and making emergency landings. This photograph shows members of 9./JG 52 in the East with Lt. Hermann Graf (fourth from the right), Uffz. Steinbatz (third from the right) and the Staffelkapitän, Oblt. Franz Hörnig (centre), who was also acting Gruppen-kommandeur

*BELOW*: The scene at Belaya-Tserkov airfield on 30 August 1941, home of I. and III./JG 3, after an attack in which Russian bombers destroyed eight Bf 109s and severely damaged two more. At this time, both Gruppen each possessed only a few aircraft and were operating together as a way of maintaining strength. This attack was therefore a severe blow for JG 3.

37-victory ace *Oblt.* Kurt Sochatzy was brought down in a Soviet air-to-air ramming, a *taran*, and taken prisoner. Awarded the *Ritterkreuz* on 12 August, Sochatzy remained in Soviet captivity until released in September 1947.

In early August, *Stab* and I./JG 53 were withdrawn from the Eastern Front, leaving their aircraft to JG 3, but at the same time, III./JG 52 arrived from Rumania. Stationed at Belaya Tserkov, III./JG 52 fought its first combats over the Kiev area on 4 August when the names of two men, later to become among the best-known of the *Luftwaffe's* pilots, first began to appear on III./JG 52's victory board. *Oblt.* Günther Rall, *Staffelkapitän* of 8./JG 52 achieved his fifth, six and seventh victories when he shot down three I-16s on the first mission of the day and during the same flight, *Lt.* Hermann Graf of 9./JG 52 achieved his first victory, also an I-16. Three days later, III./JG 52 reached its 100th victory, one of the main contributors to this success being *Ofw.* Josef Fernsebner of 8./JG 52 who was himself shot down and killed shortly after scoring his 15th victory on 9 August. By that time, the battle of encirclement at Uman had ended with a German victory and more than 103,000 Soviet soldiers marched into German confinement. Now the emphasis was on Kiev, where the Red Army would be dealt its greatest single defeat in history.

*ABOVE*: This early Bf 109 F, 'White 3', belonged to 7./JG 52.

*RIGHT*: Bf 109 F-4s of III./JG 52 in the Summer of 1941.

# June-December 1941

*THIS PAGE:* This Bf 109 E-7 of II./JG 77 was shot down in the Tiraspol area in June 1941. After examination by military personnel, who also removed the armament and other items of equipment, the remains were set on fire. Although the cowling on this aircraft might be thought to have been yellow on account of it being a lighter tone than the green of the fuselage camouflage, it should be noted that on smooth surfaces even dark paints reflect a great deal of light and can easily seem lighter than is the case. It is for this reason that, in the accompanying profile, this aircraft has been depicted with a green cowling.

## Messerschmitt Bf 109 E 'Yellow 3' of II./JG 77, June 1941

Although an early casualty of the Russian campaign, the original 71/02 scheme on this aircraft, either an E-4/B or an E-7, has already been replaced with an overall Green 70 or 71. Given the date that this machine was lost, undersurfaces were probably Blue 65 but might already have been repainted with an early example of Light Blue 76. The capped spinner is Green 71 and, as frequently observed on aircraft operated by JG 77, the yellow fuselage band has been thinly outlined in red. The emblem under the windscreen is that of II./JG 77 and the small, pale disc on the forward area of the engine cowling probably indicates a minor repair.

**II./JG 77 badge**

*LEFT:* Although it has always been supposed that the sea in the unit badge was blue, as shown here, it has been noted that an RAF A.I.2 (g) report dated 4 August 1943 mentions that the crest on a Bf 109 G-6 'White 4' of 4./JG 77, found at Soukra near El Aouina in Tunisia, is described as a "black eagle's head on white background with black sea below".

# June–December 1941

ABOVE: Contrary to popular belief, the Bf 109 was not fitted with any device for starting the engine by purely electrical means and relied on ground grew turning a handle which engaged with an inertia starter. Winding the handle turned a flywheel under the engine cowling and, once a certain speed had been attained, the engine fired. As soon as the engine started, the starter clutch was engaged by pushing in a control handle located in the cockpit and the propeller began to turn. Interestingly, the inertia starter was designed by the Eclipse company in the USA and was obtained by the German aircraft industry under licence. Here, ground staff help to start a Bf 109 F of JG 53. This particular machine is believed to have been flown by Hptm. Wolf-Dietrich Wilke, Kommandeur of III. Gruppe.

ABOVE: A Bf 109 F-2 of JG 53 at rest on an airstrip in Russia, late Summer 1941.

LEFT AND ABOVE: Lt. Franz Schiess, Geschwaderadjutant of JG 53 (LEFT) taxiing his Bf 109 F-2. This photograph is believed to have been taken on 7 July 1941 when the Stab/JG 53 claimed three SB-3s, one by Schiess, another by Major Günther von Maltzahn and one by Oblt. Hans-Joachim Heinecke. (ABOVE) A closer view of the rear of Franz Scheiss's aircraft, W.Nr. 7307, at Belaya-Tserkov on 29 July when Schiess had 14 victories. He received the Ritterkreuz on 21 June 1943 after 54 victories but was posted missing on 2 September 1943 in the Mediterranean theatre. His final victory tally was 67.

**Messerschmitt Bf 109 F-2 W.Nr. 7307 of Stab/JG 53, flown by Lt. Franz Schiess, Geschwaderadjutant, July 1941**
Although displaying a virtually standard factory camouflage finish and Stab markings, this machine is interesting as it shows the nose and spinner have been repainted. Before Operation 'Barbarossa', all aircraft of Stab/JG 53 had their spinners and engine cowlings painted Yellow 04, but this was later overpainted in the colours 02, 70, 74 and 75, as depicted in this profile. Unusually, it is believed that the kill markings on the rudder of this machine were carried on the port side only. Note the canopy framing was Green 70.

# June-December 1941

*LEFT*: Major Günther von Maltzahn, photographed on 20 July at Zhitomir after his 40th victory, is considered to have been one of the best fighter Kommodore involved in the campaign. Major von Maltzahn received the Oak Leaves on 24 July.

*RIGHT*: Surprisingly, in this photograph of von Maltzahn's rudder at least 19 victories against Western opponents are recorded whereas in fact he was credited with only 16 victories in the West in 1940 and 1941.

**Messerschmitt Bf 109 F-2 W.Nr. 8326 flown by Major Günther von Maltzahn, Kommodore of JG 53, early August 1941**
The 74/75/76 camouflage colours on this aircraft have been darkened on the fuselage with 02 and a relatively heavy application of Green 70, the original finish still showing in the area of the Hakenkreuz, which was masked off during respraying. The spinner is Green 70 with a white segment and 49 victory bars appear on the rudder. Note that the light rectangle between the Hakenkreuz and the rudder hinge line is a data plate, not an additional victory bar.

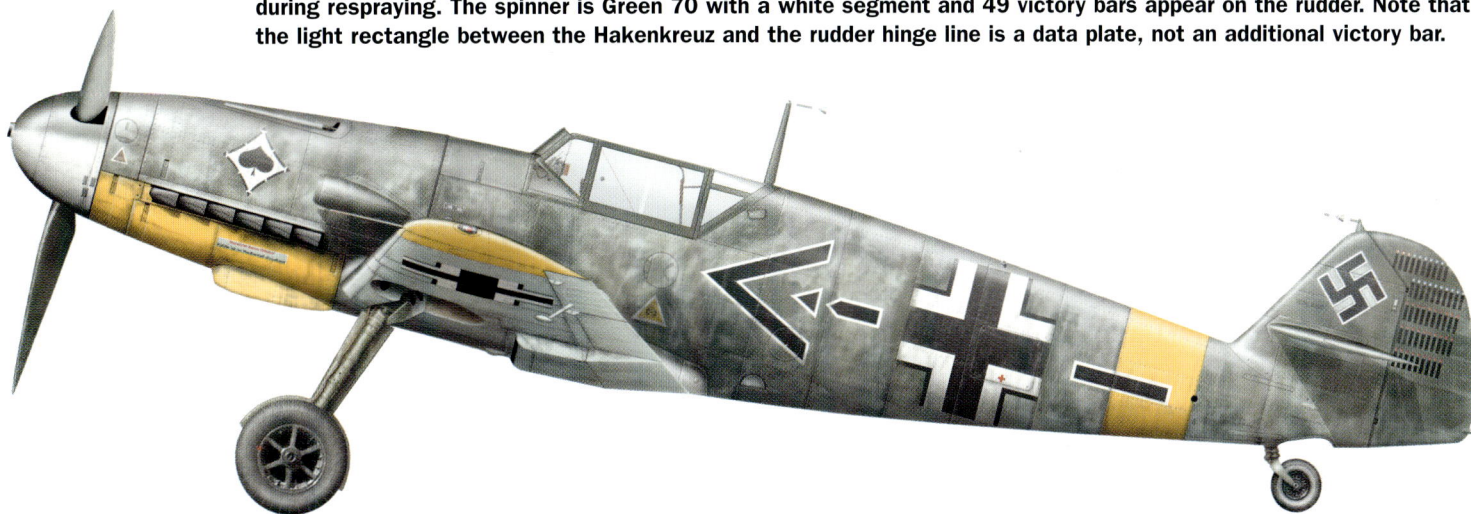

**JG 53 'Pik As' badge**

*RIGHT*: On 15 July, the cooling system of von Maltzahn's Bf 109 F-2 W.Nr. 8326, coded 'Black <<- + -', was hit and the aircraft received 30% damage when it made an emergency landing near Rzhev. Subsequently repaired, the same aircraft is seen in this photograph after von Maltzahn's 49th victory, claimed on 31 July 1941.

# June–December 1941

**Messerschmitt Bf 109 F-2, W.Nr. 5458, flown by Hptm. Hans von Hahn, Kommandeur of I./JG 3, July 1941**
The Stab markings on this aircraft are unusual but, as explained in the captions opposite, by no means unique, unlike the fuselage camouflage which consisted of remarkably concentric rings, either in 74 or, more likely 70, over Light Blue 76, which must have presented a challenge to apply neatly. The Green 25 Tatzelwurm of Stab, I./JG 3 appears on the engine cowling and a further example of neat paintwork may be seen in the green and white circles on the spinner tip. The cowling and rudder have been oversprayed to tone down the bright yellow identification colours and the victory bars represent 24 aerial victories plus three aircraft destroyed on the ground and three balloons. Note also the area of dark, heat-resistant paint applied over the wing root to protect the fuselage from exhaust staining.

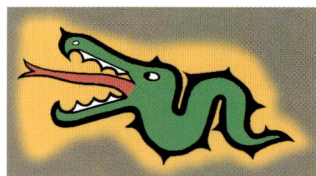

I./JG 3 badge

Personal emblem
of Hans von Hahn

Various views of the Messerschmitt Bf 109 F-2 flown by Hptm. Hans von Hahn, the Kommandeur of I./JG 3. These photographs are believed to have been taken in July 1941 when Hahn was credited with 24 aircraft destroyed in the air, three destroyed on the ground and three balloons. Hahn remained Kommandeur of I./JG 3 until March 1942 when, with a total of at least 34 aerial victories and a short spell with JG 5, he stopped operational flying and took up various staff positions and appointments in training units.

*LEFT AND ABOVE:* The Stab markings on Hahn's aircraft were also applied in an identical manner to that flown by Günther Lützow of JG 3 (*LEFT*) and the machine of JG 51 seen in the background (*ABOVE*) as Werner Mölders describes one of his air battles to Hptm. Richard Leppla, Kommandeur of III./JG 51.

*RIGHT:* 'White 8' of 1./JG 53 flying over the Eastern Front in the Summer of 1941. This particular aircraft was a Bf 109 F-2 and clearly shows the semi-retractable tailwheel which was a feature of this sub-type. In April 1942, this refinement was abandoned so that the tailwheel once more became fixed, as with the earlier Bf 109 E.

*BELOW:* 'White 1' was flown by the Staffelkapitän of 7./JG 52, Oblt. Hans Jörg Zimmermann.

*BELOW:* An early Bf 109 F of III./JG 52 running-up its engine prior to an early-morning sortie on the Russian Front. The aircraft has not been positively identified but from the yellow number just visible on the fuselage, is believed to be 'Yellow 12' of the 9. Staffel.

*LEFT*: This Bf 109 E-4/B, 'Red 5', was flown by Ofw. Reinhold Schmetzer of 8./JG 77. On Sunday, 20 July 1941, Schmetzer shot down his 20th victory, a MiG-3, but was then obliged to carry out a forced landing due to engine damage. Although the aircraft appears relatively intact in this photograph, it was assessed as 80% destroyed and written off.

**Messerschmitt Bf 109 E-4/B flown by Ofw. Reinhold Schmetzer of 8./JG 77**
'Red 5', W.Nr. 3605, was repainted in the overall Dark Green 70 or 71 scheme favoured by JG 77 and, characteristic of this unit, has also had the yellow fuselage band edged in red. The plain Green 70 spinner has a red tip, and 19 white victory bars are displayed on the rudder, the lower areas of which show where the later green has flaked away to reveal the original camouflage scheme. This earlier scheme can also be seen on the replacement panel covering the fuselage machine-guns.

III./JG 77 badge

*RIGHT*: On 1 September 1940, Oblt. Eberhard Bock was the appointed Staffelkapitän of 3./JG 3 and in that year claimed eight victories. In this photograph, taken about 10 July 1941, Bock is seen on his return from his 200th Feindflug, during which he claimed his 19th and 20th successes. On 10 August 1941, Bock's Bf 109 F-2 was hit during combat with a Russian fighter near Vassilikov, but he was unhurt and subsequently increased his total score to 21 victories before his Gruppe was subsequently transferred to the West where it became II./JG 1. This photograph shows well the soft-edged uppersurface colours.

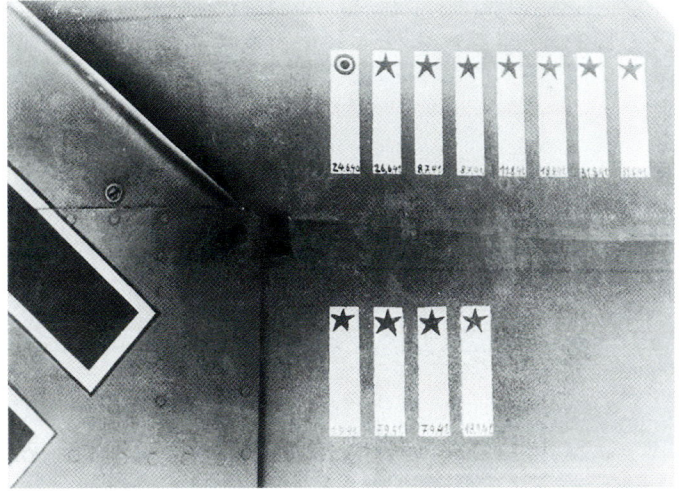

*THIS PAGE*: Bf 109 F-4 'White 8' of 7./JG 52 being made ready for another sortie in Russia. The rudder on this aircraft was marked with 12 victory tabs, the first dated 24 June 1940 while the first over a Russian aircraft was dated 26 June 1941. It is believed that this aircraft is the one in which Fw. Werner Stapel was killed when it crashed due to engine trouble on 16 October 1941.

**Messerschmitt Bf 109 F-4 'White 8' of 7./JG 52**
Finished in a camouflage scheme of 74/75/76, the colours on the wing uppersurfaces of this aircraft, W.Nr. 7017, have soft demarcation lines rather than being hard-edged and angular. The fuselage has been resprayed to include a heavy mottle of Green 70 and the cowling, originally yellow overall, has been covered with camouflage colours leaving only the lower section still yellow. Note also that the emblem of III./JG 52 on the forward fuselage has also been partly obscured and that the usual red cross on the fuselage access panel is missing. The freshly applied white tip to the Green 70 spinner contrasts with the weathered white segment.

# June-December 1941

*ABOVE AND RIGHT*: On 2 July, Oblt. Wolfdieter Huy, the Staffelkapitän of 7./JG 77, claimed his sixth and seventh victories. Three days later, while based at Iasi in Rumania, Huy was awarded the Ritterkreuz.

*ABOVE AND RIGHT*: Huy's Ritterkreuz was awarded mainly for his exploits in May when, as a Jaboflieger during operations against Crete, he had carried out several successful attacks on shipping, as indicated by the silhouettes on the rudder of his aircraft. Huy's aircraft, a Bf 109 F-4 coded 'White 1', W.Nr. 8334, remained in action until 7 June 1942 when, while on the strength of II./JG 77, it was completely destroyed after another pilot baled out and the machine crashed.

**Messerschmitt Bf 109 F-4 'White 1' flown by Oblt. Wolfdieter Huy, Staffelkapitän of 7./ JG 77, July 1941**

A number of units operating in the East seem to have preferred a dark green camouflage scheme in place of the 74/75/76 factory finish, a practice which appears to have been particularly favoured by JG 52 and JG 77. This aircraft, W.Nr. 8334, has received just such a scheme and has been resprayed with Green 70, the lower fuselage sides being further darkened by exhaust deposits. The rudder decoration shown here is just one of several variations seen on aircraft flown by this pilot.

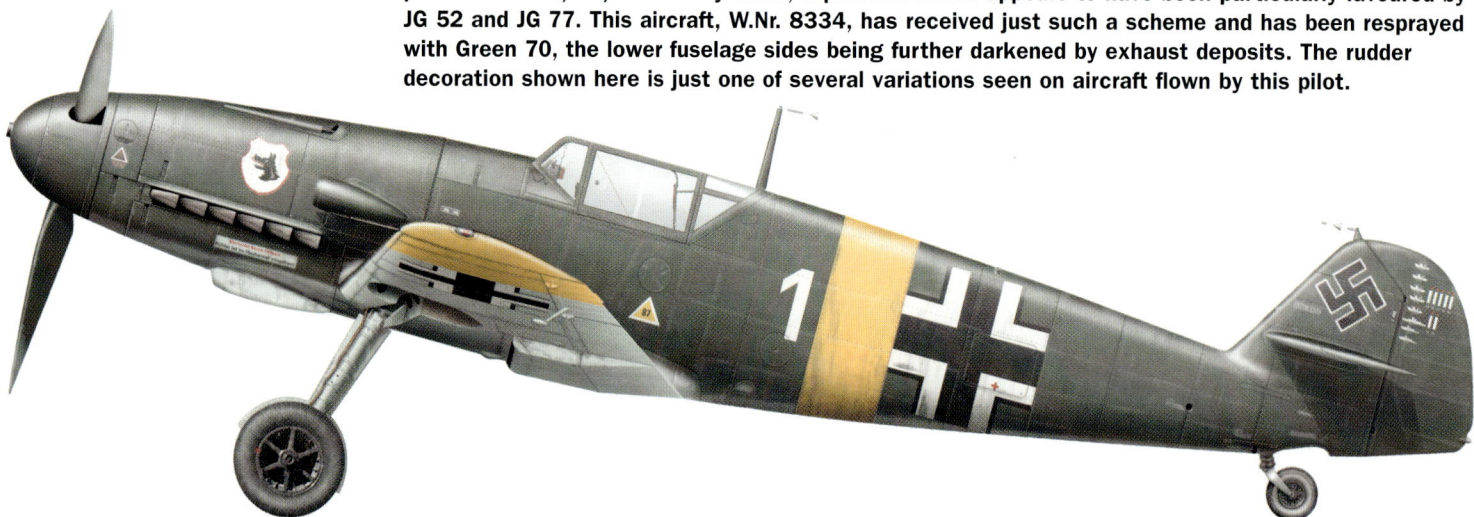

June-December 1941

Photographs of aircraft from III./JG 77 show that this Gruppe's machines appeared unusually dark as a result of the standard factory finish being overpainted with a dark green. This is particularly well shown in the photograph (*ABOVE*) depicting a Bf 109 F equipped with a drop tank in which the camouflage contrasts noticeably with the canopy framing and appears almost as dark as the 70 spinner and propeller blades. Other photographs of the Gruppe's aircraft taken in mid-1941 also show the Werk Nummer in a pale, masked-off rectangle, which confirms the aircraft were certainly repainted. Appearing slightly less dark is the finish on 'White 6', seen taxiing (*LEFT AND BELOW*). This view shows the unusually small tactical numbers employed by some Staffeln of JG 77. Note also the yellow theatre band around the rear fuselage and the row of victory bars on the rudder.

# June-December 1941

*LEFT AND ABOVE*: 'Black 2' of III./JG 77 is believed to have clipped a hedge while landing and came to rest balanced on its nose. On this aircraft, the tactical number '2' has been outlined in white, the yellow theatre markings are confined to the fuselage band only and three white victory bars were painted on its rudder. This view (*LEFT*) shows also the accumulation of oil streaks on the fuselage undersurface.

*RIGHT*: An Fw 58 'Weihe' of III./JG 77 at Iasi in July 1941. The Gruppe had at least one of these aircraft which was actively employed during the campaign against Crete. Once 'Barbarossa' had begun, this aircraft was again kept busy, particularly over the Black Sea area, searching for missing pilots and eventually returning them to their unit.

# Messerschmitts Over Smolensk

By the end of June, Army Group Centre had pinched off a Soviet salient at Bialystok and by 9 July had put an end to Soviet resistance in the Minsk pocket, capturing nearly 300,000 prisoners, 2,500 tanks and 1,400 artillery pieces. German forces continued their advance and by 16 July had broken through to Smolensk, but Soviet counter-attacks temporarily prevented German forces from completing another encirclement. There then followed almost three months of bitter fighting as the Soviets launched wave after wave of new air and ground forces against Army Group Centre's drive towards Moscow. These Soviet attempts were strategically successful, but the cost to themselves was extremely high.

Operating over this area of the front was one of the *Luftwaffe's* most successful *Jagdgeschwader*, JG 51, led by *Obstlt.* Werner Mölders, the *Luftwaffe's* highest-scoring ace. On 5 July, Mölders brought his victory tally to 86 [6] by shooting down two SBs and two MiG-3s. The MiGs are believed to have belonged to 401 IAP, an élite unit of test pilots posted to the Smolensk area on 1 July and commanded by Hero of the Soviet Union *Podpolkovnik* (Colonel) Stepan Suprun. Suprun declared he wanted to "test the German aces", but in fact the unit's MiG-3s proved inferior to the Bf 109 F-2 and the hardened veterans in JG 51 were more than a match even for the skilled fliers of 401 IAP. Indeed, on 4 July, Suprun himself was killed in combat with JG 51.

In their attempts to stop the German advance, all types of Soviet aircraft were committed against *Luftflotte* 2 and Army Group Centre, from modern Yak-1s, Il-2s and Pe-2s to the most obsolete types. On 6 July, IV./JG 51's *Lt.* Heinz Bär, one of Mölders' most promising pilots, claimed two "Severskys" which were probably Il-2s from Ground-Attack Regiment 4 ShAP, the first unit to bring this formidable ground-attack aircraft into combat. On 9 July, Mölders' claimed two elderly I-153 biplane fighters as his 87th and 88th victories and, next day, encountered two of the

The buzzard's head emblem of JG 51 first appeared early in 1941 and was, therefore, still relatively new when this photograph was taken in June.

even older, very slow and weakly armed R-Z reconnaissance biplanes which now served as light bombers. On 11 July, when JG 51 claimed 34 kills against four aircraft lost, *Lt.* Bär reached his 40th victory when he destroyed two DB-3s. Meanwhile, *Ofw.* Heinrich Hoffmann of IV./JG 51 shot down two Pe-2s as his 16th and 17th victories.

In total, JG 51 achieved more than 200 victories during the first 12 days of July, and on the 12th, III./JG 51's *Gruppenkommandeur, Hptm.* Richard Leppla, was credited with bringing down the *Geschwader's* 1,200th victory, of which 509 had been achieved on the Eastern Front. Since the beginning of the Russian campaign, JG 51's combat losses were 24 Bf 109s destroyed, 22 severely damaged and eight pilots lost, but this *Geschwader*, too, was affected by the inadequate German supply system on the Eastern Front. During the first four weeks of the war in the East, the number of serviceable Bf 109s available to JG 51 dropped from 121 to 58, of which, Mölders noted, 26 were unserviceable simply because they lacked spare parts. In this situation, the veteran pilots became even more important and the serviceable Bf 109s were flown mainly by the most successful pilots. It was, therefore, a bitter blow when *Oblt.* Hermann Staiger, *Staffelkapitän* of 7./JG 51, was severely injured on 14 July and, two days later, the Bf 109 F-2 flown by *Oblt.* Hans Kolbow, *Staffelkapitän* of 5./JG 51, received a direct hit by anti-aircraft fire during a strafing mission. Kolbow attempted to bail out from an altitude of less than 60 feet but fell to his death. These men were two of JG 51's best officers, Staiger having 25 victories and Kolbow 27.

Meanwhile, on the 15th, Mölders had become the first *Luftwaffe* pilot to exceed a total of 100 victories but was immediately grounded by Hitler who feared that his loss would be a severe blow to German morale. At the same time, Mölders became the first recipient of the Diamonds to the Knight's Cross with Oak Leaves and Swords, and he was assigned to the post of *General der Jagdflieger*.

---

6. One hundred victories, if Mölders' 14 victories in the Spanish Civil War are included.

# June-December 1941

*ABOVE*:
Oberstleutnant Werner Mölders, photographed returning from combat on 15 July 1941 when he claimed his 100th and 101st victories. As the first pilot to reach such a score, Mölders was awarded the Diamonds, a decoration subsequently awarded to other members of the Wehrmacht but which, at that time, was specially created for him.

*ABOVE*: On 7 August 1941, Obstlt. Werner Mölders, Kommodore of JG 51, was promoted to Oberst, appointed Inspekteur der Jagdflieger in Berlin and ordered not to fly any further operational missions. Here, Mölders is seen with his successor, Major i. G. Friedrich Beckh.

*ABOVE AND RIGHT*:
Although Mölders' appointment to a Staff position meant he had to leave JG 51, he remained in contact with the operational units and is seen here at Varsovia in August or September while flying to or from the front. As noted in Volume 2, Section 4, Mölders flew several similarly marked Bf 109 Fs, and while the particular machine seen here *(ABOVE)*, retained the Kommodore markings and emblem of JG 51, note that the Abschussbalken appear only on the port side of the rudder. Evident, too, in the photograph *(RIGHT)* is the number of men anxious for a glimpse of the famous ace.

The situation on the ground was now frequently extremely confusing as there were no clearly defined frontlines over a huge area. JG 51's main mission, however, was clearly defined and called for it to fly *freie Jagd* sweeps to secure air superiority and provide air cover for the ground troops. In this role its pilots continued to find opportunities to achieve higher personal successes than ever before. One example was *Lt.* Georg Seelmann of 11./JG 51, who had flown since the beginning of the war but up until the opening of the Eastern Front had two victories. However, in the first four weeks in the East he increased his victory tally to 20 as JG 51 continued to eliminate one after another the VVS units thrown into this area. A Pe-2 squadron from Bomber Regiment 411 BAP arrived at the front on 22 July and the next day despatched half its force against JG 51's airbase at Shatalovo. All were shot down. Later that day, three of the five remaining 411 BAP bombers were shot down during a second attempt to raid Shatalovo, two of them being *Lt.* Bär's 43rd and 44th victories. In the evening of 23 July, one of 4 ShAP's new Il-2s fell as Bär's 45th kill, this Soviet unit recording a total of 55 Il-2s lost on operations by the end of July. Similarly, 411 BAP's last two Pe-2s were sacrificed on 24 July, one of them claimed as the 23rd victory of IV./JG 51's *Ofw.* Heinrich Hoffmann, the other being 4./JG 51's *Lt.* Georg-Peter Eder's tenth victory. A similar fate met 410 BAP which arrived at the Smolensk sector on 5 July with 38 Pe-2s but which by 26 July had lost 33 of them including 22 shot down by German fighters. Even though VVS Western Front received 900 aircraft as replacements during July, the VVS opposed to *Luftflotte* 2 was unable to carry out more than an average of 240 combat sorties per day during the period 10 to 31 July, during which time *Luftflotte* 2's combat sortie rate averaged 575 per day.

Unable to close the ring around Smolensk, Army Group Centre was ordered to stop its drive north-eastwards towards Moscow until the city had been completely surrounded. The main emphasis of the advance now became Army Group North, which had advanced further than either Army Group Centre or Army Group South, and the seizure of Leningrad. To secure this goal, in late July the entire VIII. *Fliegerkorps* was temporarily detached from *Luftflotte* 2 and was transferred to *Luftflotte* 1. Thus, III./JG 27 and II./JG 52 were transferred northward. On 5 August, after being aided by Army Group North, the Germans announced the encirclement of Smolensk and the capture of 310,000 prisoners, 3,205 tanks and 3,120 artillery pieces. By that time, total Soviet aircraft losses since the opening of hostilities was estimated by the Germans to be 9,082. In the intense air fighting during the period between 10 July and 6 August alone, the *Luftwaffe* claimed to have destroyed almost 3,000 Soviet

*ABOVE*: Lt. Georg Seelmann flew as Staffelkapitän of 11./JG 51 for much of 1941. He received his Ritterkreuz on 6 October after 37 victories.

*ABOVE*: On 1 August 1941, Oblt. Hartmann Grasser, seen here (centre) describing an aerial combat to Mölders, became Staffelkapitän of 5./JG 51 when his predecessor, Lt. Hans-Joachim Steffens, was badly wounded in combat with a fighter and died on 13 August 1941. A former Zerstörer pilot, Grasser had claimed six victories over France and England and on 4 September 1941, received the Ritterkreuz for his 29 victories. At the same time he was appointed Gruppen-kommandeur of II./JG 51.

*RIGHT*: An SdKfz 251/1 half-track in Russia during the early days of 'Barbarossa'. This particular vehicle has been fitted with wooden frames for firing 28 cm rocket projectiles.

# June-December 1941

aircraft – 771 by *Luftflotte* 1, 1,098 by *Luftflotte* 2, and 980 by *Luftflotte* 4. But, up to 2 August, the *Luftwaffe* also recorded 1,023 of its own aircraft destroyed and 657 severely damaged on operations on the Eastern Front.

Meanwhile, throughout most of August, Army Group Centre and *Luftflotte* 2 concentrated on clearing the confused battle situation in the Smolensk–Gomel area, where JG 51 and III./JG 53 warded off increased VVS activity, not least over the German 2nd Army's bulge at Yelnya. Between 1 and 16 August, these units were credited with the destruction of 169 Soviet aircraft against 11 combat losses, and on the 16th also, *Oblt.* Karl-Gottfried Nordmann, K*ommandeur* of IV./JG 51, attained his 40th victory.

Despite their enormous losses, the Soviets still possessed a tremendous will to resist and a relentless stream of reinforcements allowed the strength of the VVS to increase. On 18 August, I. *Fliegerkorps'* bombers and the troops of 2nd Army noted intense Soviet air activity. At this time, III./JG 53 was obliged to cease all operations because it simply had no serviceable aircraft left, and the few fighters remaining to II. *Fliegerkorps* succeeded only in destroying eight Soviet aircraft and lost two of its own. Two days later, Soviet 129 IAP reported a major success by claiming nine victories for no losses over the Yelnya Bulge.

*ABOVE*: On 1 August 1941, Oberleutnante Karl-Heinz Schnell (left) and Karl-Gottfried Nordmann, both of JG 51, were awarded the Ritterkreuz by General der Flieger Bruno Loerzer (centre), commander of II. Fliegerkorps. Nordmann, who had led IV./JG 51 since 20 July 1941, claimed his 40th victory on 16 August 1941. Schnell had 31 victories when he receives the Ritterkreuz and, in September, became an instructor.

*LEFT*: This particular Bf 109 F-2 was flown by Fw. Hermann Neuhoff of 7./JG 53 and was photographed at Lepel in early July 1941, at which time Neuhoff had 16 victories. Neuhoff went on to increase his score to 40 victories, 21 of which were achieved in Russia, but was shot down over Malta in April 1942 and was taken prisoner. By that time, Neuhoff was a pilot of some considerable experience; he was the leader of his Staffel, he had been awarded the EK I, DK in Gold, and had over 400 operational flights to his credit. Two months after being shot down he received the Ritterkreuz.

## Messerschmitt Bf 109 F 'White 2' flown by Ofw. Hermann Neuhoff of 7./JG 53

When units were ordered to restrict the yellow engine cowing to just the undersides, all manner of methods were employed. Some units completely covered the yellow with a dense camouflage finish matching as closely as possible the adjacent scheme, while others were content merely to tone down the yellow with a partial covering. On this machine, W.Nr. 6702, Green 70 or 71, or possibly Grey 74 has been used and the rudder has also been partly oversprayed leaving only the lower section yellow. The yellow fuselage band, upon which is a vertical III. Gruppe bar, is unusually wide and the canopy framing in believed to have been Green 70.

# June-December 1941

*RIGHT*: On 20 July 1941, Major Friedrich Beckh, the Kommandeur of IV./JG 51, took over from Obstlt. Werner Mölders as commander of JG 51. Beckh (seen here on the right) was succeeded by Oblt. Karl-Gottfried Nordmann (left). Here, both officers apply new rank insignia to the flying jacket of Oblt. Heinz Bär who took over from Nordmann as Staffelkapitän of 12./JG 51. By 22 July, Bär had already claimed 40 victories, followed on the 29th by his 50th. On 14 August, as the Wehrmacht's 31st recipient, he was awarded the Oak Leaves. Bär survived the war with 221 victories.

*BELOW AND BOTTOM*: Lt. Ottmar Maurer of 9./JG 51 had only a short flying career in Russia. On the second day of the campaign he destroyed six Soviet SB bombers but was shot down near Yelnya on 11 August. He made a forced landing in enemy territory and was posted missing. Here, Maurer's aircraft is examined by a Russian soldier.

# June-December 1941

These photographs show two different Bf 109 F-2s, both coded 'White 11' and both flown by Fw. Werner Bielefeld of 7./JG 51 in the Summer of 1941. Note however that among the minor differences between each machine, the Gruppe bar on the aircraft (*RIGHT*) is not spaced centrally between the Balkenkreuz and the yellow fuselage band, compared with the aircraft (*BELOW*), photographed at Bobruisk on 11 July 1941, which has a unit emblem on the yellow cowling laying on the ground and just visible between the mechanic's legs

**Messerschmitt Bf 109 F-2 'White 11' flown by Fw. Werner Bielefeld of 7./JG 51**

As a general rule, a sofly applied RLM Green 70 is indistinguishable in photographs from Grey 74, but it is believed that Fw. Werner Bielefeld's aircraft was finished in a standard 74/75/76 finish with fuselage mottles in 02, 74 and 75. The pilot's nine victory bars are shown on the fin and although the spinner and propeller blades have been seriously abraded, the newly applied yellow engine cowling and Geschwader emblem are still intact.

June-December 1941

## Toward Leningrad

Before launching the final assault against Leningrad, it became necessary for Army Group North to check its flanks. Strong forces of Soviet troops still remained in northern Estonia where there was also a strong presence of Soviet fighters which made German aerial reconnaissance in particular very hazardous. To combat the Soviet fighters, JG 54 carried out *freie Jagd* missions over Estonia and the Gulf of Riga, and during one such mission on 19 July, *Lt.* Walter Nowotny of Erg.Gr./JG 54 was shot down by a Yak-1 and came down in the sea south of the Soviet-occupied Isle of Ösel. Climbing into his one-man dinghy, Nowotny paddled away from the island and continued to do so for 52 hours. In that time, he covered a distance of 60 km and reached the coast of Estonia where he was rescued. For more than three years afterwards, Nowotny always flew wearing the same trousers he had on that day, considering them a lucky charm. On the one occasion he flew without them, on 8 November 1944, he was killed.

Meanwhile, in preparation for the forthcoming offensive against Leningrad, the bombers of I. *Fliegerkorps* were concentrated against the flow of Soviet supplies on the railways. These operations were also supported by JG 54 and on 20 July, five pilots from III./JG 54 succeeded in destroying six locomotives on the Dno-Staraya Russa section of the line and completely blocked it. Nevertheless, the problem of supply was greater for the Germans than for their opponents and by 22 July, II./JG 53 reported only six serviceable aircraft. Five days later, the *Gruppe* transferred to Germany to refit with new Bf 109 F-4s and was non-operational for three weeks. It was at this time that VIII. *Fliegerkorps* was attached to *Luftflotte* 1 from *Luftflotte* 2, bringing with it the fighter units III./JG 27 and II./JG 52.

On 27 July, *Major* Hannes Trautloft, *Geschwaderkommodore* of JG 54 and also commander of the fighter units in I. *Fliegerkorps*, was awarded the Knight's Cross. Three days previously he had scored

Photographed at Ventspils (Windau) in August 1941, this Bf 109 F 'Yellow 2' belonged to the Ergänzungs Gruppe of JG 54. Until October 1941, most of the Erg. Gruppe's aircraft were Bf 109 E-7s and it is thought that this aircraft probably came from 6./JG 54 after repairs. Prior to 'Barbarossa', on 22 May 1941, 72 trainee fighter-pilots, or Jagdschüler, were undergoing final combat training with Erg. Gr./JG 54 and, with the opening of 'Barbarossa', the training Gruppe followed JG 54 to the East and was based in East-Prussia. It took part in combat over Lithuania and Estonia and experienced victories as well as losses.

# June-December 1941

## "We had to answer to the Kommodore if a bomber was lost..."

PETER BREMER, 2./JG 54

I was a pilot with 2./JG 54 and shortly before the invasion of Russia, my *Gruppe*, I./JG 54, transferred from Jever to East Prussia. We wondered why the *Gruppe* should be moved and on the evening of 21 June 1941, the *Gruppe* was assembled before the *Geschwaderkommodore*, *Major* Hannes Trautloft. He gave us the news that on the following day we would be at war with Russia and, although I began to think about the wisdom of starting a war with such a large country, any such personal thoughts were irrelevant. We were soldiers [1] and had a duty to perform.

Between 03.00 and 04.00 hrs on 22 June, we took off to escort He 111s which were to bomb Russian airfields. The war with Russia had started. We flew many missions each day, every day, advancing rapidly and hoping for an early and successful conclusion to the war.

We flew many types of missions including *freie Jagd* fighter sweeps, our favourite type of mission, with two, three, four, or twelve aircraft, during which we had to guard against being surprised by the enemy. We also flew escort missions for formations of He 111s, Ju 88s or Stukas. The latter were committed in support of the infantry at all the hot spots on the front. Our job was to cover them from attacks from above, but they were very difficult to escort due to their slow speed and, once in the target area, they attracted a lot of extremely heavy flak.

The Russian fighters' tactics involved trying to separate our escorting fighters from their charges, some of their fighters attacking the escort while the rest went after the Stukas. JG 54 became famous among the bomber units because we could be counted on to stay and provide proper protection, whereas on the Central Sector of the front, other units allowed themselves to be separated from the bombers, became engaged in air battles and thus failed in their escort duties. In JG 54, however, we had to answer to the *Kommodore* if a bomber was lost due to an enemy fighter.

We also flew low-level attacks against trains or other ground targets. During one such mission, on 6 August 1941, our *Staffelkapitän*, *Oblt.* Reinhardt Hein, went missing when his aircraft was hit by ground fire during a low-level attack in the Luga Bay area. He was taken prisoner but no trace of him has ever been found.

Each day the *Staffel* changed its code name. My first kill was scored during the advance toward Leningrad while I was flying as '*Nelke 4*' ('Carnation 4'). We were returning to our airfield in a flight of four when I saw a single enemy aircraft, a MiG. I reported it over the radio, "Indian at nine o'clock!" 'Indians' were enemy fighters, and everyone looked to the left. The arrangement was that the first pilot there would open fire. I was the first and I closed rapidly with the MiG. The enemy pilot was apparently asleep, for he took no evasive action. As my guns were harmonised by the armourers to converge at 150 metres, I opened fire at this distance, the MiG filling my *Revi* sight. The fire from the single cannon and two MGs of my Me 109 F left nothing in the sky but a cloud of debris.

I also shot down some Martin bombers which were very slow, and on 7 July, myself and two other pilots from my *Staffel* were credited with three SB-3s shot down in three minutes. The *Rata*, of which I shot down several, was famous for being able to turn on its axis but it was very slow and we were much faster. If the enemy pilots were observant, they could turn tightly and get behind us if we attacked from behind, so we had to be careful that we were always above them. When we first met the *Ratas*, they would fly a defensive circle so that each covered the fighter in front of him. Two or three of our fighters would then fly above the circle and dive down into them, open fire, and because another in the circle would be behind them, quickly climb away. By then, the circle would begin to break up and the Russians would dive in order to try to escape. However, this was their downfall since they were slower and we could then attack them from behind. The Russians did not use this tactic for very long.

We named the Il-2 'Iron Gustavs' on account of their heavy armour and, although they were very slow, they were difficult machines to destroy. We used to fly up behind them and riddled them full of holes until we thought that they would no longer be able to fly, but they did. We could even use up our entire supply of ammunition and still not score a kill. On 11 October 1941 I saw one of these machines attacking our infantry near Lake Ladoga. I decided to attack it as it approached the Newa River because I did not want to fly over enemy territory and also because I wanted to attack from the side, so avoiding the rear which was very well protected. This proved successful and the Russian was destroyed. In total, I shot down seven or eight Il-2s during my flying career in Russia.

---

1. In Germany, all servicemen are soldiers, regardless of their arm of service. Thus, even navy personnel are considered soldiers first, rather than sailors.

his 20th victory against an SB bomber. On 30 July, *Oblt.* Hans Philipp, *Staffelkapitän* of 4./JG 52 achieved his 50th victory by downing five Soviet aircraft and on 1 August, 7./JG 54's *Lt.* Max-Hellmuth Ostermann shot down a DB-3 as JG 54's 1,000th victory. However, immediately following this success, the Staffel was attacked by two Soviet fighters which set Ostermann's Bf 109 on fire and shot down *Oblt.* Günther Scholz, both pilots being lucky to escape alive.

On 6 August, *Oblt.* Reinhardt Hein, *Staffelkapitän* of 2./JG 54, was shot down and captured by Soviet troops but, on the same day, *Oblt.* Hubert Mütherich and *Oblt.* Josef Pöhs, both of 5./JG 54, were awarded the Knight's Cross for 31 and 28 victories respectively.

# June-December 1941

*LEFT*: Major Hannes Trautloft, right, the Kommodore of JG 54, in discussion with Generaloberst Keller, CO of Luftflotte 1. The aircraft in the background coded 'Black 1' is probably the Bf 109 F-2 flown by Oblt. Hubert Mütherich, the Staffelkapitän of 5./JG 54.

*RIGHT*: Oblt. Hubert Mütherich, Staffelkapitän of 5./JG 54, was in action since the campaign in Poland and had eight victories in the West and two in Yugoslavia before beginning his impressive run of victories in Russia. On 6 August 1941, Generaloberst Keller, CO of Luftflotte 1, presented him with the Ritterkreuz for 30 victories but, little over a month later, on 9 September, Mütherich was killed while making a forced landing.

*LEFT*: Lt. Josef Pöhs, one of the great aces of 5./JG 54, was also awarded the Ritterkreuz by Generaloberst Keller. Pöhs had seen action in Poland, had seven confirmed victories in the West and one in Yugoslavia. By the time of this photograph, taken on 6 August 1941, he had 28 victories scored in 225 war flights. Soon after receiving the Ritterkreuz, Pöhs became an instructor and was later involved in the initial operational flight testing of the Me 163. He was killed on 30 December 1943 when the Me 163 he was flying crashed and exploded.

# June-December 1941

*RIGHT AND BELOW LEFT*: Standing in front of the Bf 109 F flown by Hptm. Dietrich Hrabak are Oblt. Hubert Mütherich, Oblt. Hans Philipp, Hrabak and Lt. Josef Pöhs. As is evident from the way they are wearing their Knight's Crosses, Mütherich and Pöhs have just received their decorations. The long ribbon seen here and (*BELOW LEFT*) was used only during the award ceremony, after which it would be cut to length and worn under the collar. In this view, the aircraft is Mütherich's and on the day he received the Ritterkreuz, awarded for 30 victories, his score had already increased to 37.

*RIGHT*: Oblt. Hans Philipp, Staffelkapitän of 4./JG 54, photographed at Jamra Lake, on or about 6 August 1941. Philipp, who had one confirmed victory in Poland, two in Yugoslavia and 25 in the West, had already been awarded the Ritterkreuz when the war against Russia started and, by the time of this photograph, had already shot down 57 Russian aircraft. On 24 August 1941, Hptm. Philipp became the eighth member of the Wehrmacht to be awarded the Eichenlaub after 62 victories. By the end of 1941 his total had risen to 72 and by March 1942 he had claimed his 100th.

The intended final offensive against Leningrad opened on 8 August, but heavy rain and reinforced Soviet defence forces slowed the German advance. When the skies cleared on 10 August, large-scale air fighting took place above the slowly advancing *Panzer* columns with *Luftflotte* 1 carrying out 1,126 sorties while the VVS flew 908 in the same sector. II./JG 52 lost four Bf 109s on 10 and 11 August but, generally, it was the German fighters that were the masters of the air, destroying most of the 54 Soviet aircraft claimed by *Luftflotte* 1 on 10 August. On 12 and 13 August, *Major* Trautloft's fighters were credited with 35 victories for no losses of their own and, on the 14th, *Oblt.* Erbo *Graf* von Kageneck of III./JG 27 shot down five Soviet aircraft. Two days later, as the strategically important city of Novgorod fell into German hands, *Graf* von Kageneck increased his total score to 45.

JG 54's first ace killed on the Eastern Front was *Ofw.* Georg Braunshirn with 13 victories, shot down and killed on 16 August. Three days later, *Luftflotte* 1's fighter force was again strengthened when II./JG 53 returned from Germany after re-equipping with Bf 109 F-4s and started flying operations in the Lake Ilmen area. That day, *Oblt.* Hans Philipp's 4./JG 54 achieved its 200th victory, a higher number than any other *Jagdstaffel*. A few days later, *Oblt.* Philipp himself brought down his 62nd enemy aircraft and was awarded the Oak Leaves.

*BELOW*: Ofw. Georg Braunshirn of 8./JG 54, killed in combat over Kingisepp on 16 August 1941.

*LEFT*: Officers of II./JG 54. From left to right: Oblt. Hans Philipp (Staffelkapitän of 4./JG 54 since 26 August 1940, Ritterkreuz on 22 October 1940); Hptm. Dietrich Hrabak (Kommandeur of II Gruppe since 1 August 1940, Ritterkreuz on 21 October 1940); Oblt. Franz Eckerle (Staffelkapitän of 6./JG 54, which before 'Barbarossa' often operated as a Jabo Staffel, and Oblt. Hubert Mütherich, since 18 November 1940 the Staffelkapitän of 5./JG 54.

*ABOVE AND RIGHT*: This 'White 1' was flown by Oblt. Reinhard Seiler, Staffelkapitän of 1./JG 54 who, in addition to his nine victories claimed in Spain, shot down his 20th victory on 15 August (*ABOVE*) and his 21st (*RIGHT*) on 16 August 1941. The machine with the Stab markings in the background (*ABOVE*) was assigned to the Kommandeur of I./JG 54 although, interestingly, it is not clear who this was as the normal Kommandeur, Hubertus von Bonin, was apparently not in Russia at this time.

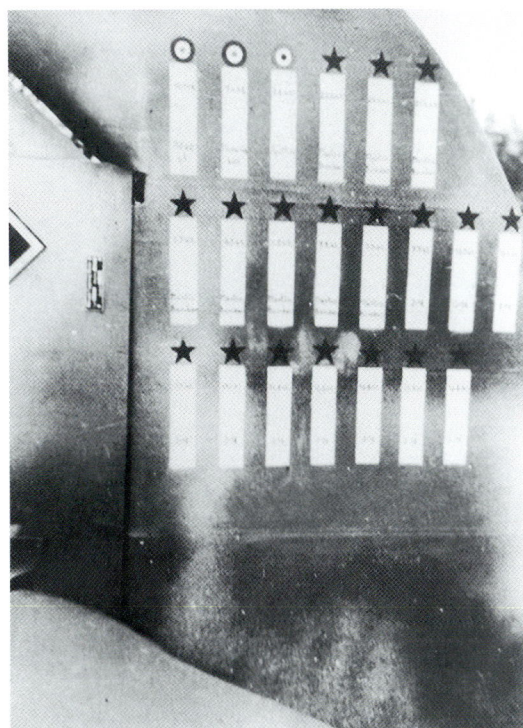

# June-December 1941

To the north of Lake Ilmen, a fierce battle raged as the Soviets fought to defend their main supply line from Moscow to Leningrad. II./JG 52 was in the forefront of these battles and lost two Bf 109s on 19 August. On the 22nd, *Lt.* Gerhard Barkhorn of 4./JG 52, later to become the second-most successful pilot in history with 301 confirmed victories, shot down what was recorded as a "Vultee 11", probably an Il-2, as his fifth victory. On the 26th, Barkhorn's *Staffelkapitän, Oblt.* Johannes Steinhoff, shot down two aircraft and two more on the 27th, receiving his Knight's Cross shortly afterwards.

*RIGHT*: During the opening weeks of the war against Russia, JG 52 committed only its II. Gruppe to the conflict. This Bf 109 F-2 'Yellow 7' of 6./JG 52 was flown by Lt. Gerhard Barkhorn and was photographed at Suwulski on 22 June 1941 after his first mission in the East. Barkhorn had joined the 6. Staffel in August 1940 and, although he flew 21 missions against England, he had no victory claims and, on 29 October 1940, was shot down into the Channel and spent some hours in the water before being rescued. Despite this inauspicious start, he finished the war as the Luftwaffe's second-highest scoring ace with 301 victories.

*LEFT*: Another view of Barkhorn's 'Yellow 7', now at Spass Main Pollis in July. Note the unusually wide fuselage band aft of the Balkenkreuz and the emblems of the Geschwader and 5. Staffel under the windscreen.

*LEFT AND RIGHT*: This Bf 109 F-2, W.Nr. 6770, was normally flown in Russia by Oblt. Johannes Steinhoff, the Staffelkapiän of 4./JG 52, but was written off in a taxiing accident at Andrejewo on 31 July. It is believed, however, that Steinhoff was not at the controls on this occasion. The victory bars show Steinhoff's eight successes in the West and the 12 claimed in the East up to the time this photograph was taken. Note the unusually glossy finish to the horizontal tail surfaces. The latest two victory bars have yet to have their red stars applied, but the stencil which will be required for this purpose may be seen between the tins of paint.

On 27 August, II./JG 54 and III./JG 53 each attained their 500th victories and about this time, IV./JG 51 was transferred to *Luftflotte* 1, increasing further the pressure on the VVS. *Oblt.* Karl-Gottfried Nordmann, *Kommandeur* of IV./JG 51, achieved his 50th victory on 28 August and his wingman, *Uffz.* Franz-Josef Beerenbrock, reached his 40th kill by downing three Soviet aircraft on 30 August, the same day that *Oblt.* Heinz Bär of 12./JG 51 shot down six. Between 20 and 30 August, Soviet fighter corps 7 IAK of Leningrad's air defence lost 52 of its 150 fighters, yet still the Soviets resisted strongly and inflicted losses. *Lt.* Georg Seelmann of 11./JG 51 shot down a DB-3 as his 36th victory on 30 August, but was rammed later the same day by a Soviet bomber. Seelmann baled out over Soviet-controlled territory but managed to evade capture and returned to the German lines. Bär had a similar experience after scoring his 79th and 80th victories against two Pe-2s on 31 August. His 'Black 1' was shot down behind enemy lines but despite two sprained ankles, Bär also returned to the German lines. III./JG 53's *Lt.* Erich Schmidt was less fortunate. With 47 victories, Schmidt was the most successful pilot in III./JG 53 but when his 'Yellow 6' was shot down by ground fire on the 31st, Schmidt baled out over Soviet-controlled territory and was never seen again. Three days later, III./JG 53 was moved south to participate in the offensive against Kiev.

*ABOVE AND RIGHT*: Oblt. Heinz Bär of IV./JG 51 was awarded the Ritterkreuz on 2 July 1941 for 27 air victories. By 18 August, just six weeks later, his tally has risen to 60 and he was awarded the Eichenlaub. Soon afterwards, on 31 August 1941, he shot down two Pe-2s as his 79th and 80th victories but was obliged to make a forced landing behind enemy lines. At the time, Bär was flying a Bf 109 F coded 'Black 1', possibly the aircraft shown here (*RIGHT*), although with only two victory bars, this is clearly not the machine he normally flew. Although both his ankles were sprained in the emergency landing, Bär quickly abandoned his machine and hid himself to avoid detection by Soviet troops who arrived to examine the aircraft. He then remained concealed until the following morning when, endeavouring to disguise himself as a Russian peasant, he succeeded in returning to the German lines. Bär then spent the next two months in hospital recovering from the effects of walking on his injured ankles.

### Messerschmitt Bf 109 F-2 'Black 1' of IV./JG 51
The camouflage on this aircraft consisted of the standard 74 and 75 uppersurfaces with 76 undersurfaces and fuselage particularly finely mottled with 02, 70 and either 74 or 75. The spinner was 71 overall and the original yellow engine cowling and rudder had both been oversprayed to provide a more effective camouflage. A IV. Gruppe symbol was applied aft of the fuselage Balkenkreuz and a strip of red primer had been applied to the fuselage under the windscreen, presumably where some minor repair had been carried out. Two black victory bars appeared on the rudder.

# June-December 1941

*RIGHT*: During July 1941, I./JG 3 lost ten Bf 109s during operational sorties over the Eastern Front. One of these was flown by Ofw. Heinz Schmidt of 3./JG 3 who took off on the 20th to attack Soviet observation balloons in the Kiev area but was shot down by anti-aircraft fire. Although Schmidt was captured, his subsequent fate is unknown and he was posted missing. Here Soviet troops examine Schmidt's aircraft, a Bf 109 F, W.Nr. 8980, coded 'Yellow 4'.

*LEFT AND ABOVE*: Lt Erich Schmidt of III./JG 53 received the Ritterkreuz for 30 victories on 23 July 1941. He is seen here (*LEFT*) standing on the wing of a Bf 109 F-2. A short time later, on 31 August, by which time he had 47 victories, Schmidt was posted missing near Dubno.

Among the last successes achieved by IV./JG 51 on the Northern Front were two SBs brought down on 8 September by *Ofw.* Heinrich Hoffmann as his 54th and 55th victories. Soon afterwards, the *Gruppe* transferred to Army Group Centre to help suppress the increasing Soviet air activity in that sector of the front.

As the German *Panzer* troops closed in on Leningrad in early September, the ground fighting grew even harder. At the same time, the *Luftwaffe* was forced to re-locate some units to other sectors of the front at the very time the Soviets transferred new units, including seven fresh fighter regiments, to the Leningrad sector. The inevitable result was that *Luftflotte* 1 received a series of severe personnel losses. On the 6th, II./JG 52 lost the 30-victory ace *Oblt.* August-Wilhelm Schumann when his 'Black 1' crashed near Lyuban. On 9 September, 5./JG 54's *Staffelkapitän,* 43-victory ace *Oblt.* Hubert Mütherich, was shot down by Soviet fighters and was killed when he attempted to belly-land his badly damaged 'Black 10'. When the Germans made a fruitless attempt to break through Leningrad's defence perimeters on 11 September, there were severe losses on both sides. Although JG 54 recorded 17 victories against three losses and II./JG 53 claimed nine, this latter *Gruppe* lost *Ofw.* Stefan Litjens (24 victories) when he was shot down and severely injured. III./JG 27 also claimed nine kills on 11 September but lost *Lt.* Hans Richter (21 victories) when he was shot down by an I-16; and on 19 September, III./JG 27 lost *Fw.* Ernst Riepe (six victories) who went missing in his 'Yellow 11' after an aerial combat. Six days later, *Ofw.* Franz Blazytko (30 victories) of III./JG 27 was captured after being shot down, possibly by *M.Lt.* (Junior Lieutenant) Dmitriy

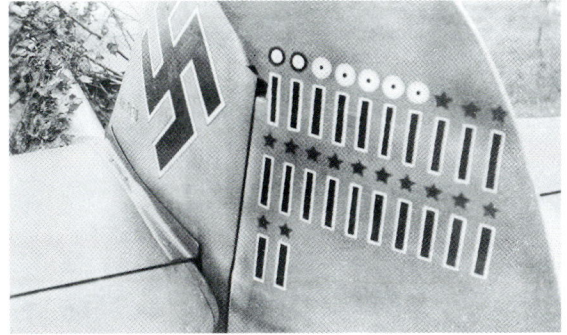

*ABOVE*: Rudder of Ofw. Stefan Litjens' Bf 109 F-4, W.Nr. 7173, 'White 5' of 4./JG 53, marked with 22 victory bars and photographed at Lyuban on the day he was injured, 11 September 1941.

# Through forest, marsh and swamp

GERHARD PROSKE, I./JG 54

At around 10.15 hrs on 27 October 1941, the 1./JG 54 engaged a number of Soviet J-26s (I-26s) in combat. After I had shot down one of them in the vicinity of Tichwin, my aircraft was attacked by another Russian fighter and sustained numerous hits. With a seized engine and a coolant temperature of 160°, I was forced to crash-land my Me 109 on its belly in a snow-covered marsh near a tall, dense forest in Soviet territory, approximately 30 km. south-east of the bridgehead. As I climbed out of the cockpit, I saw in the distance numerous Russian soldiers with rifles advancing rapidly in my direction. Because I had to escape to safety immediately, I therefore had no time in which to retrieve the emergency rations from the fuselage of my Me 109. The Russians fired at me and, crouching to make myself as small a target as possible, I hurried towards the cover of the trees and concealed myself so that the Russian soldiers were unable to discover me. Later, under the protection of darkness and with the assistance of my compass, I headed west through forest, marsh and swamp.

Even during the night, because the snow and trees formed a strong contrast, I was able to maintain a straight course, but my pilot's fur-lined boots were heavy and wet due to wading through the snow and my feet were stiff. During the day I hid and rested, but I did not sleep for fear of freezing to death. It was very cold and, from time to time, I performed all kinds of exercises to keep warm. On the second day, my pilot's fur-lined boots were heavy and wet due to wading through the snow and my feet were stiff and very painful. By the third and fourth days I had lost all feeling in them.

To add to all this misery I suffered from hunger and thirst. I had nothing to eat, nothing to drink and nothing to smoke, so I had to sustain myself for four days without food, liquid and tobacco. On the first day I had felt little hunger and cold, but on the second and third days I thought I would collapse. Occasionally I ate some snow to satisfy my thirst, but the march through the snow tested me severely and due to my exhaustion I was able to make only slow progress. I began to feel an indifference which reached its height on the fourth day. Oddly, this feeling came on at night when everything was quiet, but as soon as I heard the sound of combat, new courage and hope reappeared and I wanted to return to my comrades!

During the fourth night, I reached a forest near the village of Petrowskoja. I waited there until dawn approached, since I did not know for certain if I was within German or Russian lines. That morning, under cover of the trees, I crawled toward the sound of a firing artillery piece. When I was about 100 metres from this gun, I recognized a Russian guard, and as I pulled back, I noticed two more Russian soldiers behind their machine-gun. I crawled along this machine-gun's line of fire and thus toward the German lines. At the same time, I heard the firing of the German machine-guns but I could not make out the German troops as they were well-camouflaged in their white coats. I moved toward the explosions of the Russian shells and finally, on the evening of the fifth day, reached a German battery. At last I was safe.

Two German infantrymen brought me to Petrowskoja where my frozen feet were bandaged and I finally received something to eat and drink. That night, I slept on a plank bed, but it seemed like heaven. On the following day, I was brought to Tschudowa in a army personnel vehicle and ten days after my emergency landing I was reunited with my comrades of the 1. *Staffel*. I was home!*

---

* On 30 January 1944, by which time Proske had been promoted to *Feldwebel*, he was again forced to land on the other side of the lines due to engine failure. On this occasion, however, he fell into Russian captivity and it was not until September 1949, after five years of harsh conditions as a prisoner of war in the Urals, that Proske returned home to Germany.

# June–December 1941

*LEFT*: As the nose of this aircraft of JG 54 completely obscures the pilot's view ahead, the risk of a collision while taxiing on dusty, crowded airfields was lessened by having members of the ground staff seated on the wings to guide the pilot.

*LEFT*: Soviet troops examining the Bf 109 F-2 'Black 1' in which Oblt. Reinhardt Hein was shot down on 6 August 1941. Hein, the Staffelkapitän of 2./JG 54, was captured slightly injured.

*RIGHT*: Hptm. Reinhard Seiler, Staffelkapitän of 1./JG 54. In the background is his Bf 109 F marked with Stab symbols and a Mickey Mouse emblem, a souvenir from his time with the Legion Condor.

*LEFT*: A member of the ground staff with Hptm. Reinhard Seiler's rudder when he was Staffelkapitän of 1./JG 54. Not recorded here are Seiler's nine victories in Spain, the victory bars starting with two French aircraft and a Spitfire, the latter destroyed on 5 August when Seiler was also severely wounded. Almost exactly a year later, on 15 August 1941, Seiler claimed his 20th victory and his rudder is shown here shortly afterwards marked with 21 bars. The odd striped effect over the Hakenkreuz is believed to have been on the original print but its significance is not known.

*LEFT AND BELOW*: Mechanics at work on the Bf 109 F-2 flown by Lt. Max-Hellmuth Ostermann of 7./JG 54, probably in August 1941. Later, this machine was repainted *(BELOW)* and by the Autumn of 1941, when Ostermann's 33 kill markings were recorded on the yellow rudder, the band ahead of the fuselage Balkenkreuz had been positioned as a backing to the cross. This in turn allowed the number '2' to be repositioned closer to the cross.

*BELOW*: Lt. Max-Hellmuth Ostermann (centre, facing camera) surrounded by fellow officers. Ostermann joined 7./JG 54 in April 1940 and claimed two victories during the French campaign, six during the Battle of Britain and one in the Balkans. In Russia, he quickly became one of the most successful pilots and was one of the best at aerial combat manoeuvres despite being so small that wooden blocks had to be added to his rudder pedals. He is seen here shortly after receiving the Ritterkreuz which was awarded on 4 September 1941 when he had 29 victories.

*LEFT*: Ostermann, on the right, with the rudder of his machine, now marked with more than 40 victory bars.

**III./JG 54 badge**

**Messerschmitt Bf 109 F-2 flown by Lt. Max-Hellmuth Ostermann of 7./JG 54**

Lt. Ostermann's 'White 2', W.Nr. 5485, is shown here as it appeared in the Autumn of 1941 when the pilot had 33 victories. The camouflage finish consists of the standard 74/75/76 scheme with the fuselage mottled in 74 and 75 and yellow theatre markings in the usual areas. The tip of the Green 70 spinner is in black and white, the badge of III./JG 54 appears under the cockpit, and the winged clog emblem of 7. Staffel is painted on the cowling.

**Variation of 7./JG 54 badge**

# June-December 1941

*RIGHT*: Uffz. Fritz Zander of 5./JG 54 on the wing of his 'Black 1'. The name 'Lia' under the cockpit refers to his wife, Elise. Note that, as appropriate for this period, the colour for the second Staffel within a Gruppe is black and, indeed, the Staffelkapitän, Oblt. Hubert Mütherich, is known to have flown 'Black 10'. Later in the war, Zander transferred to Reichsverteidigung duties where he flew with JG 1. The lines painted on the canopy side windows were used as an aid to bomb-aiming. On the Northern Front, an inadequate number of standard bomber aircraft prevented large-scale attacks against ground targets and it therefore became especially important to commit fighter aircraft as fighter-bombers. During the winter months, JG 54 carried out a number of trials to determine the suitability of the Bf 109 in this role. Best results were achieved by attacking at an angle of 45 degrees from 2,000 to 3000 metres, as the aircraft attained a high speed which exploited the element of surprise and the high velocity of the bombs ensured greater accuracy. Another advantage was that the aircraft remained within range of ground fire for only a short time. By comparison, low-level attacks resulted in losses disproportionate to success. During fighter-bomber operations in the Winter of 1941, six of the seven aircraft which JG 54 lost were due to ground fire encountered during low-level attacks. In addition, 36 aircraft were hit in their radiators, only a few of which could be flown back to their operational airfield and safely landed.

*ABOVE*: Twenty-nine years old Hptm. Franz Eckerle, the Staffelkapitän of 6./JG 54, posing with the rudder of his Bf 109 F at Siverskaya. Before the war, Eckerle had been famous for his aerobatics and had won many flying contests in Germany. He claimed two victories in France but, because the 6. Staffel became a Jabo unit during the latter stages of the Battle of Britain, was able to claim only two more over England. Once in Russia, however, his tally rapidly increased and he is seen here in September 1941 after being credited with 30 victories.

*ABOVE*: On 18 September, after approximately 35 victories, Hptm. Eckerle was awarded the Ritterkreuz and on 6 January 1942 he became Kommandeur of I./JG 54. Shortly afterwards, on 14 February 1942, Eckerle made a forced landing in enemy territory and was posted missing. With a total of at least 59 victories, he was awarded the Oak Leaves in absentia.

June-December 1941

In the Autumn of 1941, Uffz. Peter Bremer of 2./JG 54 flew two Bf 109 Fs, both coded 'Black 12' and both named "Hermännchen", or "Little Hermann". These photographs (*LEFT AND BELOW LEFT*) show, however, that the position and presentation of the name differed on each machine. On both aircraft the original camouflage finish has been considerably modified to lighten it. On the aircraft seen (*LEFT*) with a mat protecting the walkway areas on the wing, all but the most meagre traces of the original splinter pattern have been oversprayed leaving only small patches of the original 74/75 scheme to produce a mottled effect. An almost identical effect may be seen on this group of Bf 109 Fs (*BELOW*) photographed in a hangar in Russia. Unfortunately, the unit is this case is not known, but 'White 3' in the centre of the picture has a row of white victory bars painted under the Hakenkreuz on the fin, a position known to have been favoured by JG 53.

**Messerschmitt Bf 109 F-2 'Black 12' flown by Uffz. Peter Bremer of 2./JG 54, Autumn 1941**
Named 'Hermännchen', this aircraft's original 74/75/76 scheme has been modified with a random pattern of mottles in 79, 02 and 70 in order to improve its camouflage against the seasonal colouring. The pilot's six victories are recorded on the rudder in the usual way, but more unusual are the red and white warning stripes on the pitot tube.

# June-December 1941

*LEFT*: A severe loss for JG 54 occurred on 30 September 1941 when the Bf 109 F-2 flown by Hptm. Arnold Lignitz, Kommandeur of III./JG 54, lost a wing during combat over Leningrad, possibly by a rocket fired from an I-153. It is thought that although Lignitz survived this incident, he later died in one of the city's jails, probably from starvation. In this connection, it must be remembered that when the German Army reached Leningrad on 1 September, Hitler ordered that, to avoid German losses, the city was to be besieged. It was subsequently cut off from all land communications and subjected to air and artillery bombardment. Before the end of 1941, starvation was causing 300 deaths a day and by the time the siege was eventually lifted, in January 1944, an estimated one million inhabitants had died as a result of disease, starvation or enemy action. It is therefore hardly surprising that if the population was unable to feed itself, it was certainly unable to feed a prisoner. Lignitz, who had 25 victories at the time he was shot down, was promoted Major after his capture and was replaced by Hptm. Reinhard Seiler.

Tatarenko of the independent fighter squadron 13 OIAE/VVS KBF. Finally, on 30 September, III./JG 54's *Gruppenkommandeur, Hptm.* Arnold Lignitz, was shot down over Leningrad by an I-153. Lignitz, a *Ritterkreuzträger* credited with 25 victories was held by Soviet troops in Leningrad where he died.

Despite the loss of many of *Luftflotte* 1's best fighter pilots, however, the *Luftwaffe* fighter arm remained superior in airmen and aircraft. The Soviet situation was incomparably worse, and of the 445 pilots available to 7 IAK on 1 July 1941, this number had dropped to 88 three months later. Nevertheless, the stiff Soviet defence and the German Army's inability to bring forward replacements and spare parts to its first-line units made it impossible for the Germans to achieve their goal of capturing Leningrad. Eventually, they decided not to assault Leningrad but to besiege it and starve it into surrender. Thus, from late September, when VIII. *Fliegerkorps* returned to *Luftflotte* 2, JG 54 remained as the only fighter unit in *Luftflotte* 1.

*BELOW*: A Rotte of Bf 109 Fs from 2./JG 54 flying over the Leningrad area, Autumn 1941.

*ABOVE*: Uffz. Alfred Grislawski pictured with his Bf 109 F-4 'Yellow 9'. Grislawski made his first claim on 1 September 1941.

*RIGHT*: Snow-camouflaged 'Black 2' of 2./JG 54. This aircraft was photographed by Uffz. Peter Bremer while the Rotte was engaged in a freie Jagd sweep over the Volkhov front.

## Annihilation at Kiev

After the successful conclusion of the battle of encirclement at Uman in the Ukraine during the first half of August 1941, German Army Group South concentrated its forces against the mighty Dnieper River in the east, and by 23 August had seized its first bridgeheads at Zaporozhye, Cherkassy and Gornostaypol. This drive was supported from the air by *Luftflotte* 4, which mustered the fighter units *Stab*, I., II. and III./JG 3; *Stab* and III./JG 52; *Stab,* II. and III./JG 77; and I.(*J*)/LG 2.

Meanwhile, Army Group Centre's 2. *Panzergruppe*, commanded by *Generaloberst* Heinz Guderian, opened a major offensive to the south from its positions in the Gomel area, 130 miles north of Kiev, with the aim of meeting up with Army Group South and trapping the entire Soviet South-Western Front in a huge pincer manoeuvre. Initially, Soviet opposition against Guderian's attack was weak and the heavy losses in the air during the past weeks had reduced the strength of the VVS to less than one hundred aircraft.

Control of the air cover over Guderian's troops was the responsibility of II. *Fliegerkorps*, but JG 51 achieved only two aerial victories in the first two days of the offensive. Soviet reinforcements in the form of a complete army group, *General-Leytenant* Andrey Yeremenko's new Bryansk Front, were rushed in to meet Guderian's offensive with an air force mustering 464 aircraft, but the bulk of VVS Bryansk Front's airmen lacked combat experience, were inadequately trained, and relatively few of the aircraft they manned were of the latest models. The VVS units of the Bryansk Front first went into action on 25 August and during a battle with MiG-3s and bombers, *Hptm.* Hermann-Friedrich Joppien, *Kommandeur* of I./JG 51, was killed. With 70 victories to his credit, Joppien was the *Luftwaffe*'s fourth-ranking ace at the time of his death. Despite this loss and the numerical superiority of the VVS Bryansk Front, the quality of the *Jagdwaffe* pilots compared with their Soviet opponents was such that JG 51 soon established air superiority and on 27 August claimed 35 victories for no losses. Thus VVS Bryansk Front was already crushed when, on 3 September, III./JG 53 arrived from *Luftflotte* 1. On 8 September, the *Kommodore* of JG 51, *Major* Friedrich Beckh, was credited with the *Geschwader's* 2,000th victory, more than 1,300 of which had been achieved since 22 June 1941.

This Bf 109 F-2 was flown by Hptm. Wilhelm Hachfeld who took over I./JG 51 in October after the death of Hptm. Hermann-Friedrich Joppien. Hachfeld, who had previously led the Gruppe's fighter-bomber Staffel, 2./JG 51, was one of the Luftwaffe's Jabo specialists. He left I./JG 51 in May 1942 and was instrumental in the creation of the dedicated Jabo Gruppe III./ZG 2 which was subsequently in action in North Africa.

Further south, the air fighting over Army Group South increased in intensity as the Soviets attempted to suppress the increasing number of German bridgeheads on the Dnieper's eastern bank, but again the main result was further losses in the Soviet air units. The 13 September was a particularly dramatic day, JG 3 claiming 25 Soviet aircraft shot down including 13 "V-11s", probably Il-2s, for the loss of one Bf 109 over the bridgehead at Kremenchug. Twenty of these kills were claimed by II./JG 3 and the *Geschwaderkommodore*, *Major* Günther Lützow, contributed by bringing down two DB-3s for his 69th and 70th victories. Also on this day, I./JG 3's last three serviceable Bf 109s carried out their final combat sorties before the *Gruppe* was withdrawn to Germany where it was eventually redesignated II./JG 1.

As the *Panzer* groups from Army Groups South and Centre converged, forming the jaws of the war's greatest pincer movement, the lines of retreat where Soviet troops tried to escape entrapment were attacked by hundreds of German bombers from *Luftflotte* 2 and *Luftflotte* 4 while Bf 109s from five *Jagdgeschwader* kept the skies clear of opposition. On 16 September, 1. and 2. *Panzergruppen* met at Lokhvitsa, 130 miles east of Kiev, and closed the ring around five Soviet armies. The final stage of the Kiev battle was characterised by complete German control of the air and between 17 and 26 September, JG 51 recorded a total of 41 victories, with JG 3 claiming 35 and III./JG 53 claiming 14. When the battle was over, 440,000 Soviet soldiers had been taken prisoner in the collapsed Kiev pocket.

# Friedrich Beckh

## Early Career

**F**riedrich Beckh was born in Nürnberg on 17 January 1908. Although his early years, and also those of his brother, Wilhelm, were marred by the premature death of their mother, they were fortunate to find in their father's second wife a good stepmother who also gave them a stepbrother. After completing his *Abitur,* or school leaving examination, Friedrich Beckh entered the then 100,000-man strong German Army in 1926 and joined the cavalry. There, in spite of his height and weight (he was nearly two metres tall, weighed almost 100 kg and wore size 47/48 shoes) he succeeded in becoming one of the best riders in his unit and participated in many riding competitions. Beckh, however, had always been attracted by the thrills and risks associated with speed and, shortly after the official creation of the *Luftwaffe,* he asked for a transfer to the still-expanding German Air Force. Officially integrated into the *Luftwaffe* with the rank of *Oberleutnant* in 1935, he started flying training and, simultaneously, began to enter air rallies and races where soon he again became well known for his skill. Later, he also developed an attraction for elegant sports cars and his men became accustomed to see him arrive at his airfield in these splendid vehicles.

Naturally, in view of his character, Beckh opted to fly fighter aircraft and, despite his unusual height and weight, was posted to JG 134 in 1936. Nevertheless, at the beginning of the war, because he was then over 30 years of age, he did not take part in any war flights and was sent instead to the *Luftkriegsschule* where he occupied different positions in the General Staff. It was probably there that he met Werner Mölders, with whom he became a close friend and whose operational experience in the Spanish Civil War was often cited in the different levels of authority within the *Jagdwaffe.*

On 27 July 1940, *Major* Mölders became *Kommodore* of JG 51 and, shortly afterwards, he arranged for *Hptm.* Beckh to transfer to that *Geschwader,* Beckh arriving in October as an officer detached from the General Staff. At the year's end, Beckh was promoted *Major i.G.* and, at the same time, I./JG 77, which had for several weeks been under the command of JG 51, officially became IV./JG 51, so making JG 51 the first *Jagdgeschwader* to possess four full *Gruppen.* On 16 February 1941, the *Kommandeur* of IV./JG 51, *Hptm.* Johannes Janke, left the unit to take over a position in the *Stab* of a *Nachtjagddivision* and, while awaiting a new, official *Gruppenkommandeur, Oblt.* Hans-Karl Keitel, formerly *Staffelkapitän* of 10./JG 51, was meanwhile selected to lead the *Gruppe.* Although it was unusual to have an *Oberleutnant* in a position normally occupied by a *Major,* or at the very least by a *Hauptmann,* Mölders had chosen to appoint Keitel, who then had eight victories, in accordance with Göring's wish to have only experienced and successful pilots in positions of command. However, Keitel's tenure as acting *Kommandeur* was brief as he was killed in action on 26 February 1941 and Mölders was again faced with the problem of appointing a successor.

Friedrich Beckh was an expert horseman and was a successful entrant in many equestrian events.

With a height of 190 cm, or 6 ft 2 ins, a weight of around 95 kgs, or 209 lbs (almost 15 stone) and wearing size 48 shoes, Beckh's height and size was unusual for the time, as shown in this photograph (*BELOW LEFT*) where he towers above his colleagues. His physique made it as difficult for Beckh to cram himself into a sports car (*BELOW CENTRE*) as it did to lever himself into the cockpit of a Bf 109 (*BELOW RIGHT*).

## Beckh is Appointed Kommandeur

Beckh prepares for a sortie in the Winter of 1940/41. In the photograph (*BELOW*) he is passing his spectacles to a member of his ground crew for safe keeping while the view (*BELOW RIGHT*) clearly shows the aircraft's yellow nose. Note also the glossy appearance of the Stab markings against the matt camouflage finish.

It was under these circumstances that *Major i.G* Friedrich Beckh proposed that he should himself become *Kommandeur*. He had the requested rank, had for a long time been seeking action and, despite already being 33 years of age, felt he had the skills of a 20 year old. Moreover, as a staff officer, he possessed all the theoretical knowledge necessary to lead a *Gruppe*. However, besides his age and physical size, Beckh's eyesight had deteriorated since he had joined the *Luftwaffe* in 1935 and by 1941 he had to wear spectacles. Although Mölders finally accepted the solution and officially named Beckh as *Kommandeur* of IV./JG 51, he certainly had his doubts about Beckh's abilities and ensured that he would always be escorted by an excellent *Rottenflieger* with sufficiently good eyesight to serve both the *Kommandeur* and himself.

Accordingly, on 5 March 1941, when IV./JG 51 became involved in its first action since the loss of Keitel, *Major* Beckh was escorted by the former *Legion Condor* member and later *Ritterkreuzträger*, *Ofw.* Adolf Borchers, who flew as his wingman. In this action, Beckh was able to claim his first victory, a Spitfire shot down from an altitude of 8,200 metres in combat off Boulogne, while Borchers also claimed a Spitfire. A few days later, on 10 March, Beckh claimed his second victory north of Le Touquet and, on 6 May, with the excellent *Oblt.* Karl-Gottfried Nordmann as his wingman, he claimed another Spitfire as his third victory. His fourth, a Hurricane, fell on 21 May.

**Messerschmitt Bf 109 E-4 flown by Major i.G Friedrich Beckh, Kommandeur of IV./JG 51, March 1941**
Major Beck's aircraft is believed to have been finished in a scheme consisting of mixed greys approximating the later shades 74 and 75 with additional 02 and 70 mottles on the fuselage sides. Apart from a single victory bar on the fin, representing a Spitfire shot down on 5 March 1941, no personal decorations are carried and the Kommandeur's chevrons on the fuselage sides and the yellow recognition markings of the period are standard.

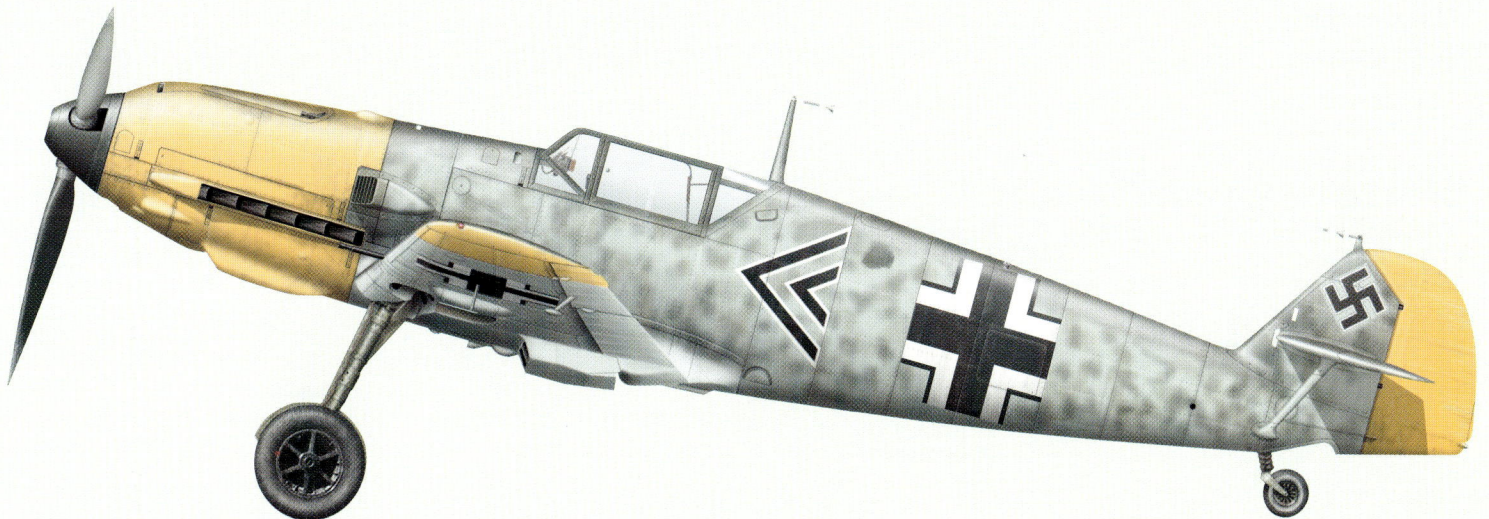

*RIGHT*: Major i.G. Beckh's aircraft in flight.

*BELOW*: Major i.G. Beckh with ground personnel. His aircraft carries a single victory bar on the fin representing his first claim; a Spitfire on 5 March 1941. Note the red stripes on Beckh's trousers indicating an officer of the Genereralstab.

## Geschwaderkommodore

During the first months of Operation *'Barbarossa'*, *Major* Beckh became very successful and, on 21 July 1941, was finally chosen by Mölders to succeed him as *Kommodore* of JG 51. Beckh's place as *Kommandeur* of IV./JG 51 was taken by *Oblt.* Karl-Gottfried Nordmann and the new *Kommodore* also attracted to his *Stab* another famous pilot, the Austrian *Lt.* Bernd Gallowitsch of 12./JG 51, who at that time was credited with about 20 victories and who flew as Beckh's wingman. Soon, the Beckh-Gallowitsch team proved most successful and on 8 September 1941, Beckh claimed JG 51's 2,000th victory.

Beckh's luck turned for the first time on 16 September when, during a low-level mission, his Bf 109 F-2 was hit by flak. Although badly wounded in his left foot, Beckh survived and, two days later,

he was awarded the *Ritterkreuz*. By this time, he had been successful in 27 combats, including his four in the West, and had also destroyed about 20 Russian aircraft on the ground. Although his wound temporarily prevented him from flying further missions, he continued to lead his *Geschwader* from the ground until, on 3 October, he finally had to resign himself to enter hospital in order to avoid the risk of infection in his wounded foot. *Jagdgeschwader* 51 then came under the command of *Major* Günther Lützow who, for a while, led his own JG 3 as well as JG 51. Having temporally lost his *Rottenführer*, 'Gallomir' Gallowitsch returned to 12./JG 51 where he soon claimed his 40th victory.

Apparently, in early 1942, Beckh was again able to fly missions and claimed approximately 20 more victories before he was posted back to the *Reichsluftfahrtministerium*. His successor as *Kommodore* of

*BELOW*: Ground personnel servicing Beck's Bf 109 F in Russia.

JG 51 was, once again, the same *Major* Nordmann who, six months earlier, had succeeded Beckh as *Kommandeur* of IV./JG 51. However, Beckh's new position in the *RLM* certainly did not please him and soon he was pressing to be returned to the front. He was granted his wishes when, on 3 June, following the death in action of *Major* Wilhelm Lessmann, he was named *Kommodore* of JG 52.

Beckh, however, scored no more victories. On 21 June 1942, he took off in a Bf 109 F-4 coded 'Black 4' for a fighter sweep against enemy airfields, the kind off mission he particularly liked. He was accompanied on this occasion by the experienced *Ofw.* Berthold Grassmuck who subsequently wrote the following report:

*Grassmuck Oberfeldwebel, 1./JG 52*

*In the field, 28 June 1942,*

*At 09.35 on 21.6.42, I took off as wingman to Major Beckh in order to carry out a fighter sweep in the area of Isjum-Kupjansk-Waluiki. I observed a Russian air base east of Waluiki. With Major Beckh, I circled over the landing field three times at an altitude of 3,000 metres.*

*Afterwards, Major Beckh headed down to 1,000 metres toward another enemy landing field which was covered with Russian fighters. Then nine LaGG-3s came towards us. Immediately Major Beckh attacked the aircraft in front and shot it down. The pilot baled out. During the dogfight other LaGG-3s took off so that there were about 20 Russian fighters in the air. During the air battle the flak discharged a heavy concentration of fire. After the first kill Major Beckh attacked another aircraft. During the air combat, numerous LaGG-3s attacked Major Beckh from the rear. I was able to shoot down one of these aircraft. When it was no longer possible for me to cover Major Beckh, I called out on the radio, "Ten enemy fighters behind us." Major Beckh pulled up at a shallow angle and was able to shake off the Russian fighters. As we were pulling up, I saw the detonations of four flak bursts directly under Major Beckh's aircraft. Afterward it trailed white smoke. I called out over the radio, "Head for own lines, aircraft emits white trail of smoke." Since I received no answer from Major Beckh, I repeated this message. The aircraft continued to fly in the same direction for about 50 seconds and then nosed down and dived into the ground at a steep angle. The aircraft burst into flames upon impact. I could not circle over the crash site since there were six LaGG-3s behind me. I could not determine if Major Beckh had taken to his parachute. The crash site is about 3-4 km. SW of Waluiki…*

*(Signed) Ofw. Grassmuck*

## A Mystery Solved

On the evening of 21 June, Beckh's family listened to a radio broadcast announcing the *Heldentod*, or Hero's Death of Friedrich. The next day the family received from the *Oberkommando der Luftwaffe* an official written confirmation of his death and, for a while, there seemed little doubt concerning the certainty of his fate.

Beckh's reported death was a severe blow to JG 52 as he was the *Geschwader's* second *Kommodore* lost in three weeks. However, in view of Grassmuck's doubt about whether or not the *Major* had baled out, rumours quickly began to circulate that perhaps Beckh had after all survived the crash and had been taken prisoner. Indeed, about a week later, interrogation of a captured Russian pilot revealed that an injured German officer with the red stripes of the Generalstab on his trousers had been taken prisoner a few days earlier. When shown several photographs of Beckh, the Russian confirmed that indeed he recognised him as the officer captured earlier. This information clearly introduced an element of doubt over Beckh's fate and his loss was amended in official records from 'killed' to 'missing' in action.

Thus began the hope that Beckh may have survived and, for several years after the war, Beckh's father contacted many former pilots and made enquiries about his son. Although nothing conclusive emerged, hope that he may have survived was maintained by such letters as the following, written in 1951 by the ace Adolf Borchers:

*'[Although] I did not participate in your son's last mission, the statement of the German pilot regarding the crash of your son's aircraft cannot however be entirely accurate. Among us pilots of JG 51 'Mölders', the official version at that time was that your son received hits during a low-level attack on a Russian airfield, had to carry out a crash landing, and was taken alive into Russian captivity. This report was later supported by a statement made by a captured Russian pilot who claimed that, a few days earlier, a German Major with red stripes on his trousers had crash-landed near his airfield and had become a prisoner of war. This is consistent with the fact that your son, as a member of the General Staff, flew while wearing his staff trousers. Unfortunately, during my own period of captivity in Russia, I heard nothing further about your son.'*

*Adolf Borchers*

Eventually, as the years passed and all hope faded, Beckh was finally declared "Gefallen".[1] Then, in early 2002, the author of this biography was contacted by Russian aircraft enthusiast Evgenij Belogurov who asked if the name *Major i.G.* Friedrich Beckh was known to him. The enthusiast then explained that in 1976 he had visited the site of a crashed Bf 109 which, according to an eye-witness, had been pursued by four Russian aircraft, one of which had shot it down. The German machine had then plunged into a marsh near Waluiki, in the Belgorod province, and there, at a depth of three metres, the enthusiast had found a well-preserved body, a number of personal documents in which the name Beckh appeared several times, and a diary in which the last entry was dated 19 June 1942.

At last it was possible to inform Beckh's family and the German War Graves Service of these facts and, at the time of writing, it is hoped that Friedrich Beckh may finally receive a decent burial.

---

1. Killed in action.

# June-December 1941

**Badge of 2./JG 3**

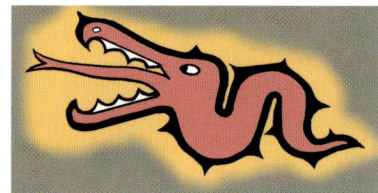

**Messerschmitt Bf 109 F 'Black 7' flown by Oblt. Helmut Meckel of 2./JG 3, July 1941**
Although in standard 74/75/76 factory finish, the fuselage sides on this machine are unusually dark where the 02/74/75 mottling has been heavily oversprayed with Green 70. The original completely yellow cowling has been toned down with a patchy overspray to bring it in line with the latest directive calling for only the cowling undersurafces to be yellow, and this machine carries victory bars on the rudder representing the pilot's claim of 22 aircraft destroyed. Canopy framing appears to have been Green 70.

*LEFT*: Bf 109 F 'Black 7' flown by Knight's Cross holder Helmut Meckel on the Southern Sector of the Eastern Front in July 1941. Meckel flew with I./JG 3 and his aircraft is shown here marked with 22 victory bars. After a crash which rendered him temporarily unfit for flying duties, Meckel later transferred to the Stab of JG 77 in North Africa but during the final days in Tunisia was killed when his Bf 108 crashed on take-off on 8 May 1943. Some uncertainty exists regarding Meckel's final total of victories, was 25.

*LEFT AND RIGHT*:
On 27 August 1941, III./JG 53 claimed 19 Russian aircraft destroyed, increasing the Gruppe's total number of victories from 496 to 515 and thereby exceeding the anxiously anticipated 500. On this occasion, (*LEFT*) a report was broadcast by the Propaganda Abteilung (note the microphone), during which the Kommandeur, Hptm. Wolf-Dietrich Wilcke, (*RIGHT*) who may himself have been responsible for the Gruppe's 500th victory, was interviewed. Wilke's claim on this occasion was his 29th.

*RIGHT*: These aircraft are believed to have been photographed after being withdrawn from the front line, either to be repaired or to be transferred. The Bf 109 F belonged to III./JG 3 but the 'Emil' parked alongside probably belonged to another unit.

*RIGHT*: Luftwaffe mechanic Gefreiter Hans Brecht of 8./JG 52 working on the fuselage of one of the Staffel's stripped-down aircraft. This photograph was taken in August 1941 when the temperature was 50°C. Barely visible is the new emblem of III. Gruppe, a barbed red cross on a white diamond, which first appeared in the Summer of 1941 and replaced the earlier running wolf design based on the name of the first Kommandeur, Major Wolf-Heinrich von Houwald. Note the application of a solid, dark colour, possibly green, applied to the fuselage.

*BELOW*: 'Black 4', a Bf 109 F-2 of 8./JG 52, photographed in the Summer of 1941. Note the tyres have been covered to protect them from the sun and that despite regulations calling for a white segment to be factory-applied to the spinner, this appears to have been omitted.

# June-December 1941

## Unternehmen Taifun

When the assault against Moscow was launched under the code-name *Unternehmen 'Taifun'*, or Operation *'Typhoon'*, it marked the decisive stage of *'Barbarossa'*. By 30 September 1941, the *Luftwaffe* had claimed a total of 14,500 Soviet aircraft destroyed, including approximately 5,000 in aerial combat, whereas its own total losses on the Eastern Front between 22 June and 27 September 1941 amounted to 1,603 aircraft destroyed and 1,028 severely damaged [7]. The strength of *Luftflotte* 2 which had II. and VIII. *Fliegerkorps* under its command and which was assigned to provide air support, had dwindled from 1,200 to 549 aircraft. The fighter units participating were *Stab*, II. and III./JG 3; III./JG 27; the entire JG 51; I. and II./JG 52; and III./JG 53. Included in III./JG 27 was the first Spanish fighter unit to participate in the war, 1/o *Escuadrilla Azul*, which was designated 15.(*Span.*)/JG 27. By 27-28 September, the total strength of the whole of JG 3 amounted to just 30 serviceable Bf 109s, III./JG 27 possessed only 11 while the entire JG 51 had no more than some 50 serviceable fighter aircraft.

Operation *'Typhoon'* commenced on 30 September with an attack launched by *Generaloberst* Guderian's 2. *Panzergruppe,* later redesignated a *Panzer Armee*. On the first day of the offensive there was virtually no Soviet aerial opposition, but strong reinforcements were soon allocated to the contested area and as early as 1 October the Soviets were able to assemble 301 serviceable bombers and 201 fighters against *Luftflotte* 2, followed shortly afterwards by the fighters of Moscow Air Defence's 6 IAK which were also brought into action. A relatively large number of these aircraft were of the latest types; MiG-3, LaGG-3 and Yak-1 fighters, Il-2 ground-attack aircraft and twin-engined Pe-2 bombers. Meanwhile, more *Luftwaffe* units were withdrawn to rest and refit, II. and III./JG 53 leaving in early October. Despite the diminishing number of serviceable aircraft, this may have been quite a sound decision since, at that time, there were more pilots available at the front than aircraft. All aircraft and technical stocks belonging to the units that left for Germany were handed over to those that remained.

---

7. Fighter losses in this period amounted to 466 destroyed and 333 severely damaged.

# "We were simply doing our duty..."

DRAGUSTIN-KARL IVANIC, JG 52

**B**efore the war I studied and received a diploma in aircraft construction. Croatia was an autonomous state within Yugoslavia and we became independent in 1941. I became a reserve lieutenant and flew the Me 109 B together with various other Yugoslavian fighter aircraft, and when the leadership of the nation called upon us, I volunteered for the *Luftwaffe*. We were enthusiastic but at that time we did not know what would be the ultimate outcome of the war. In the Summer of 1941, we were sent to Herzogenaurach, in Germany, for training.

In early October, we arrived at Poltava where our unit was attached to III./JG 52. Our group of 24 Croatian fighter pilots was then organised as the 15./JG 52 under the command of Colonel Franjo Dzal, and while our German colleagues were equipped with the Bf 109 F, we only had Emils. Nevertheless, our *Staffel* had at least one F but this was flown by our German attaché, Lt. Baumgarten. We spoke both German and Croatian and received the respect of the other fighter pilots of JG 52. If we were captured by the Russians, our fate would have been worse than that of the Germans as the Russians failed to understand why any nation would choose to ally itself with Germany.

I flew my first combat mission on 10 or 12 October 1941, during which there was an engagement with Russian ground-support aircraft which were attacking our infantry at low level. I was filled with anxiety but not fear, and scored a victory over an I-16 *Rata*. The I-16 was not very fast but it was very manoeuvrable and could only be brought down when surprise was achieved. Thus we attacked them and I was able to score my first kill. The first victory is not necessarily the most important kill but it enabled me to acquire some important experience. When one scores a kill, it is not a reason for celebrating the killing of another human being, at least this is how I viewed war. We were simply doing our duty, just as our opponents were also doing their duty to their country. We did, however, celebrate the awards of decorations.

At the end of October we were in Kharkov but soon left for Taganrog. It was here, on 20 November, that our German attaché collided with a *Rata* and was killed. In December 1941, we were based at Mariupol. The Winter of 1941/42 was very severe, but we were equipped with warm flight suits with fur, our rations were very good and we normally slept in permanent buildings, not tents. In such cold conditions, the main problems occurred when the engines were started, but we were fortunate and had sufficient aircraft heating equipment.

June-December 1941

On 2 October, *Oblt.* Karl-Heinz Leesmann's I./JG 52, which had transferred to the Eastern Front from Holland prior to *'Typhoon'*, made a conspicuous debut by shooting down four Soviet aircraft. The next day, JG 51 reported two victories against two losses, one of which was IV. *Gruppe's Ofw.* Heinrich Hoffmann, credited with 63 victories, who went missing in his 'Brown 2' after an air combat near Shatalovo aerodrome, possibly shot down by 233 IAP's *St.Lt.* Sergeyev. The next day, Spanish *Comandante* (Lieutenant-Colonel) Angel Salas Larrazabal achieved 15.(*Span.*)/JG 27's first two victories when he destroyed an I-16 and a Pe-2.

The air war during Operation *'Typhoon'* reached a climax on 5 October, when JG 51 claimed 20 victories without suffering any losses. Meanwhile, in JG 3, the *Geschwaderkommodore, Major* Günther Lützow, shot down four DB-3s, and II. *Gruppe's Kommandeur, Hptm.* Gordon Gollob, reached his 51st victory by downing two fighters. Lützow scored another four victories on 9 October, two on 10 October, and one on 11 October. On the latter date he became the fourth serviceman of the *Wehrmacht*, all of whom were fighter pilots, to be awarded the Swords to the Knight's Cross with Oak Leaves. The largest contribution by any single *Jagdgruppe* was that given by *Hptm.* Karl-Heinz Leesmann's I./JG 52 which, between 2 and 10 October, was credited with 58 victories against seven losses.

The Soviets now sent further reinforcements to the endangered sector, four bomber regiments arriving from the Central Asian Military District on 10 October, and all available aircraft took part in an offensive against *Luftflotte* 2's air bases. However, this operation, which commenced on 11 October and lasted for eight days, was a total failure. During this period, *Oblt.* Erbo *Graf* von Kageneck of JG 27 shot down three Il-2s on the 11th followed by a MiG-3 on the 12th, bringing his Eastern Front victories to 47 and his total victory tally to 65, for which he was awarded the Oak Leaves on 26 October 1941. Also on the 12th, III./JG 27, less 15.(*Span.*)/JG 27, left the Eastern Front and II./JG 3 left *Luftflotte* 2 and transferred south to reinforce *Luftflotte* 4 in the Crimea. On 13 October, JG 51 claimed ten victories for the loss of 7. *Staffel's Lt.* Joachim Hacker, credited with 32 kills. Next day, Soviet 10 SAD, 12 SAD and 450 ShAP attacked German columns in the Yukhnov–Spas Demensk area; 15.(*Span.*)/JG 27 reported three DB-3s shot down, two of them by *Cte.* Angel Salas Larrazabal. JG 3's *Major* Lützow claimed a MiG-3 and a DB-3 for his 96th and 97th victories.

By 7 October, large pockets of Soviet troops had been cut off around Vyasma and Bryansk, but the next day, the Autumn weather began to have an effect as heavy rains and mud began to slow German units pushing towards Moscow from the north and south. The effect on aerial operations, however, was more gradual and spasmodic, so that while *Luftflotte* 2 mounted only 51 sorties on 19 October and hardly any the next day, an improvement in the weather between 22 and 23 October allowed 939 sorties

Already loaded with four SC 50 bombs, 'White 5' of III./JG 27 was probably photographed at Dugino, north-west of Vyazma, at the time of the first snowfall in early October 1941. Soon after this, in mid-October, III./JG 27 and the Geschwaderstab were withdrawn from the Russian Front to Döberitz for re-equipment. Between about 20 November and mid-December 1941, the flying elements were transferred to join I. Gruppe, which had established itself in North Africa in April 1941, and II. Gruppe, which had also transferred to Africa between the end of September and the end of October.

to be flown. However, the subsequent air battles also showed that the VVS was improving and in those two days, although JG 51 claimed 17 victories, it sufferred five losses including 7. *Staffel's Ofw.* Robert Fuchs, credited with 23 victories, and 1. *Staffel's* 12-victory ace *Ofw.* Heinz Schawaller.

The next day, JG 3's *Major* Günther Lützow carried out two missions. Shortly after 10.30 hrs, he engaged a small group of MiG-3s and shot down one, his 99th victory, in his first attack. There then followed a ten-minute turning combat before Lützow was able to shoot down his next MiG-3, making him the second pilot to achieve 100 confirmed victories in the Second World War. On his second mission, at 14.23 hrs that day, Lützow shot down a third MiG-3, following which he was ordered not to fly any further combat missions.

By this time, both sides had become almost bogged down in the mud some hundred miles west of Moscow. *Luftflotte* 2 did its utmost to intervene against counter-attacking Red Army units but suffered from a rapidly diminishing number of serviceable aircraft. In addition to this, conditions on the improvised frontline airstrips were frightful, and aircraft which did manage to take off were confronted by steadily mounting opposition from the VVS. The 15.(*Span.*)/JG 27 was dealt its first combat loss on 25 October when *Teniente* (Lieutenant) Abundio Cesteros Garcia was wounded in action. Two days later, 7./JG 51's *Oblt.* Herbert Wehnelt was shot down by an Il-2 shortly after achieving his 19th victory and was seriously injured.

The first five weeks of *'Typhoon'* had indeed resulted in enormous Soviet losses, the Red Army facing Army Group Centre suffering more than 650,000 casualties between 30 September and 5 November 1941. In the air war, JG 51 claimed a total of 289 victories in October against 13 Bf 109s lost due to enemy action. Actual VVS losses during the defence operations to the west of Moscow between 30 September and 5 November 1941 were 293 aircraft and many Soviet air units were badly depleted. On 29 October, 29 IAP and 187 IAP reported only two serviceable fighters apiece, while 198 ShAP was down to a single serviceable Il-2.

Between 1 October and 8 November, the *Luftwaffe* claimed to have destroyed a total of 2,174 enemy aircraft on the entire Eastern Front; 1,293 in aerial combat, 412 by *Flak,* and 469 on the ground. Although these figures reveal a considerable drop in the intensity of the air fighting, the daily average of Soviet aircraft claimed shot down in air combat now being 33 compared to 100 during the first weeks of the war in the East, they also indicate that the Soviets had learned from their previous mistakes and were taking greater care in dispersing and camouflaging their aircraft on the ground.

These photographs clearly illustrate the muddy conditions at Smolensk-Nord , the base of III./JG 51. Note that a few 'Emils' continued to serve with JG 51 in Russia until the Spring of 1942.

June-December 1941

ABOVE LEFT: Ground staff applying another victory bar to the rudder of what is believed to be the aircraft flown by Oblt. August Wilhelm Schumann, the Staffelkapitän of 5./JG 52. However, there is a discrepancy between the 45 victory bars seen in the photograph and the pilot's official total of 30; this is perhaps due to the difference in the number of victories claimed as opposed to the number actually confirmed.

ABOVE: Oblt. Schumann was killed on 6 September 1941 when he flew too low and his aircraft collided with an obstacle on the ground. Although he baled out, Schumann was too low for his parachute to open and his death was another serious blow to the Staffel which, by that time, had already lost half its pilots either killed, wounded or missing in action in Russia.

ABOVE: On 27 September 1941, I./JG 52 left its bases on the Dutch coast and set out for Ponyatovka to join the rest of the Geschwader in Russia. Here, in October, a number of the Gruppe's Bf 109 F-2s undergo final armament checks, 'Black 1' being possibly the aircraft flown by the Staffelkapitän of 2./JG 52, Oblt. Robert Göbel.

RIGHT: The Bf 109 F-2 'Yellow 5' flown by Lt. Gerhard Barkhorn of 6./JG 52, photographed in the Autumn of 1941. Note the wide yellow band after the Balkenkreuz and that although the aircraft lacks both Staffel and Geschwader emblems, the name "Christl" has been applied under the cockpit. By the end of 1941, Barkhorn had ten victories.

# June-December 1941

Major Hanns Trübenbach (*ABOVE LEFT*) led JG 52 from 19 August 1940 to 10 October 1941. (*ABOVE*) Another view of Trübenbach, centre, showing his Bf 109 F-4 and (*BELOW*), the same machine as it taxies out prior to another sortie. It was quite usual for commanding officers to be allocated more than one aircraft, the reserve machine sometimes bearing identical markings or, as seen here (*LEFT*) with variations. In this case, the yellow band is in a slightly different position and, as was common practice in JG 52, a feint number '2', believed to have been green, has been added to the Stab markings.

**Messerschmitt Bf 109 F-4, W.Nr. 7079, flown by Major Hanns Trübenbach, Kommodore of JG 52, October 1941**
The original 74/75/76 factory finish on this machine has been completely resprayed Green 70 with evidence of the earlier scheme remaining only around the fuselage Balkenkreuz and a masked-off rectangle containing the W.Nr. on the fin. A completely yellow cowling has been retained and the position of the yellow fuselage band ahead of the Balkenkreuz is unusual but by no means unique. The Green 70 spinner lacks the usual white segment.

**JG 52 badge**

# June-December 1941

*RIGHT*: A Bf 109 F-4/B of III./JG 52. This aircraft probably belonged to the 8. Staffel which operated in he Jabo role and would normally have flown with an ETC under the fuselage.

*LEFT* A line-up of Bf 109 F-2s of II./JG 51 in the Autumn of 1941. Note the position of the horizontal II. Gruppe bar which has been applied between the fuselage cross and tactical number. This practice was characteristic of JG 51 and continued until 1944.

(*BELOW LEFT*) Photographed at Shatalovo on 11 August 1941, this photograph shows the Bf 109 F flown by Erich Hohagen, Staffelkapitän of 4./JG 51, after his 25th victory. Soon after this photograph was taken, Hohagen received the Ritterkreuz on 5 October 1941 after 30 victories. Hohagen later flew with JG 2 and JG 26 on the Channel Front and was finally with JG 7 and JV 44.

(*BELOW RIGHT*) Another successful pilot who flew with 4./JG 51 was Otto Schultz whose first victory came on 22 June 1941, the opening day of 'Barbarossa'. His aircraft is seen here at Staraya-Bykow on 26 July with 11 victory bars. Later, Schultz was awarded the Ritterkreuz and survived the war with 73 victories. Note again the position of the Gruppe bar.

# June-December 1941

*ABOVE*: Stab markings on a Bf 109 F-2 of JG 51 in Russia, early Autumn 1941.

*BELOW*: Bf 109 F-2, 'Brown 4', of 12./JG 51, in the Autumn of 1941.

*ABOVE*: Two Bf 109 Fs seen under repair, or perhaps being cannibalised, during the Autumn of 1941. In the background, 'Black 8' of IV./JG 51 has had its engine removed and the rudder of the aircraft in the foreground has been damaged. Note also the eight victory bars on this machine, all recording earlier kills in the West.

*BELOW*: Waffen-SS soldiers inspecting a Bf 109 F-2 belonging to Stab/JG 53 after a successful forced landing. In October 1941, when JG 53 left the Russian theatre of operations, it had suffered six pilots killed in action, seven missing, two PoWs and 26 wounded . In return, JG 53 claimed a total of 769 victories in Russia, mostly by the III. Gruppe which claimed approximately as many as the I. and II Gruppen combined.

*ABOVE*: Flying with Stab III./JG 53 was Lt. Jürgen Harder (above left), brother of the famous Hptm. Harro Harder who, with 11 victories, had been one of the most successful pilots of Legion Condor.

*THIS PAGE*: Lt. Jürgen Harder, seen here (*ABOVE LEFT*) with his parents, probably at Mannheim-Sandhofen shortly before transferring to the East, claimed his tenth victory on 25 September 1941 but on the same day he became disoriented and, short of fuel, was obliged to put down his unusually marked aircraft (*ABOVE AND BELOW*) in a forced landing near Novgorod. Fortunately, Harder escaped unhurt and went on to receive the Ritterkreuz on 5 December 1943 and the Oak Leaves on 1 February 1945. He was killed in action on 17 February 1945, at which time he was credited with 64 victories.

### Messerschmitt Bf 109 F flown by Lt. Jürgen Harder of Stab III./JG 53, Summer 1941

This aircraft, W.Nr. 8085, is finished in standard 74/75/76 colours but with any 02 and 70 mottling being confined to the rudder area and the yellow nose, the latter having been oversprayed to make it less conspicuous. What sets this machine apart from other aircraft of the period, however, are the wing uppersurfaces, which appear to be in a single colour, and the unusual Stab markings, the exact significance of which are not known. Jürgen Harder's first ten victories were all claimed in Russia, although here only a single victory bar representing his first, an I-16 which he shot down on the afternoon of 22 June 1941 is shown. The name which appears under the cockpit commemorates one of this pilot's brothers, Harro Harder, who as Kommandeur of III./JG 53 was killed on 12 August 1940.

*ABOVE AND RIGHT*:Two views of the Bf 109 F flown in Russia by Major Günther Lützow, the Kommodore of JG 3. In the photograph (*ABOVE*) the aircraft is undergoing armament harmonisation while in the photograph (*RIGHT*) Lützow's machine is seen behind 'Spatz".

## Messerschmitt Bf 109 F-2 flown by Major Günther Lützow, Kommodore of JG 3, Summer 1941

**Standard 74/75/76 camouflage appears on this aircraft with the fuselage mottled in 02, over which are further mottles of 74 and 75 slightly darkened with Green 70. Yellow theatre markings are carried, and the Stab marking, a triple chevron, is that of the Geschwaderkommodore.**

*ABOVE AND ABOVE RIGHT*: Already a holder of the Oak Leaves, Major Lützow (far left) was awarded the Swords on 11 October 1941, at which time he had been credited with 92 confirmed victories, and had a final total of 108.The machine depicted in the profile is devoid of any Abschussbalken or unit identity, although at least one of Lützow's aircraft carried victory bars, as confirmed by these photographs which are believed to have been taken after Lützow's 101st victory on 24 October 1941.At that time, however, while retaining command of JG 3, Lützow was also serving as interim commander of JG 51 while the Kommodore of that unit, Major Beckh, was recovering from wounds.The victory bars may therefore have been applied to Lützow's aircraft only for the short time he was with JG 51.

## Over Kharkov and the Crimea

Meanwhile, Army Group South had launched attacks to capture Kharkov and secure the Ukraine. After the Battle of Kiev in mid-September 1941, *Luftflotte* 4's forces were dispersed between three main targets; the Soviet industrial centre in Kharkov and the Donets Basin; the Crimea; and Rostov. Since JG 3 had been transferred to *Luftflotte* 4 to participate in Operation *'Typhoon'*, *Luftflotte* 4 could muster only four *Jagdgruppen* for these tasks, namely III./JG 52, which was transferred to Poltava in the eastern Ukraine to support the drive against Kharkov, and II. and III./JG 77 with I.(*J*)/LG 2 which were in action on the right flank of Army Group South.

Despite its numerical inferiority, after about ten days of intense aerial activity, III./JG 52 managed at least to achieve local air superiority. During this period, *Uffz.* Gerhard Köppen of 8./JG 52, who had scored his first victory only on 24 June 1941, achieved his 18th and 19th victories on 24 September when he destroyed a MiG-3 and an SB; and on 4 October, Köppen's *Staffelkapitän*, *Oblt.* Günther Rall, shot down his 19th and 20th victories which were claimed as "Severskys" but which were probably Il-2s. Between 3 and 14 October, III./JG 52 was credited with more than 50 aerial victories without losing one of its own aircraft to hostile action and by 17 October, *Oblt.* Rall had already claimed his 25th victim, a Yak-1.

Nevertheless, Soviet bomber and ground-attack aircraft continued to attack the German advance columns with considerable effect and on 9 October, German 17th Army complained about *"incessant enemy aerial attacks which are most troublesome to our advance"*. Two days later, an *Armee Korps* under 17th Army reported 196 casualties as a result of the day's Soviet air attacks. This contributed largely towards slowing down Army Group South's advance. Meanwhile, in an unparalleled evacuation operation, the Soviets succeeded in dismantling and transferring eastwards 1,523 factories, installations and research establishments. This included 85 per cent of their airframe and aero-engine production facilities and was a feat which German bomber operations against rail lines in the area failed to prevent.

Farther south, an attempt in mid-September by the German 11th Army to seize the Crimean Peninsula had failed due to stiff Soviet resistance. Supported by 200 fighters and 130 bombers of VVS ChF, the Soviets managed to hold their positions on the Perekop Isthmus connecting the Crimea with the mainland. In a further attack by 11th Army on 26 September, although JG 77 and I.(*J*)/LG 2 claimed 29 Soviet aircraft shot down against two combat losses, the Soviet airmen succeeded in providing their ground troops with decisive support and this second German attack also failed to achieve a decisive breakthrough.

Most of the Soviet aircraft shot down over the Perekop Isthmus on 26 September were bombers or ground-attack aircraft, some of them biplanes, which became easy prey to Bf 109s which bounced them from above, but the situation was greatly different in pure fighter *versus* fighter combat. Among the Soviet fighter units in the Crimea was *Kapitan* (Captain) Ivan Lyubimov's 5 *Eskadrilya* (Squadron)

Although III./JG 77 was mainly equipped with the Bf 109 F, it still possessed a few 'Emils' which it continued to operate until early 1942. Here, 'Yellow 11' is being stripped of components in order to keep two other aircraft flying. 'Black 1' is thought to be the aircraft belonging to Oblt. Anton Hackl who was appointed Staffelkapitän of 5./JG 77 on 29 July 1941 and who was destined to become a leading ace.

The 8./JG 52 was commanded from July 1940 by Oblt. Günther Rall, who had scored his first victory on 18 May. Due to heavy losses during the Battle of Britain, III./JG 52 had to be withdrawn from the front to recuperate, so preventing Rall from adding to his score until the beginning of 'Barbarossa'. Rall then claimed his second victory on 24 June 1941, and subsequently became very successful, his total reaching 36 by the end of November. This photograph shows the rudder of Rall's machine at Belaya-Tserkov in the Summer of 1941, when his tally stood at 13, the last being claimed on 17 August 1941. Rall would subsequently claim his 14th victory on 30 August.

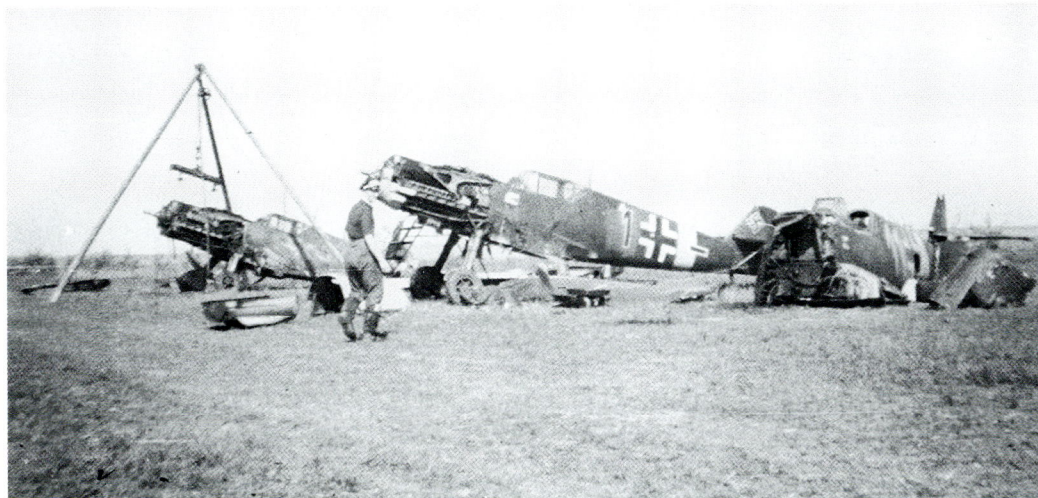

# June-December 1941

# "They had very good aircraft..."

ALFRED GRISLAWSKI, III./JG 52

I was born on 2 November 1919 and from an early age I wanted either to join the *Kriegsmarine* or become a fighter pilot. When the time came, there were too many candidates for the *Kriegsmarine* and, with the hope that I could combine both childhood dreams, I was accepted by the *Marine-Flieger*. However, I was soon transferred to a bomber-unit and this was not at all to my liking as I wanted to be a fighter pilot and not a "bus-driver". After nearly two years in different schools and non-operational units, I finally transferred to III./JG 52 near Calais. This unit had suffered heavy losses in the fighting against Britain and had to be withdrawn, first to Berlin-Döberitz and then on to Rumania.

At about this time the A/B schools were established, so I completed my training with one of these and received fighter training first at Stolp and then at the *Ergänszungsgruppe* at Merseberg. The *Ergänszungsgruppe* trained pilots on the type of aircraft we would fly in combat. Eventually, I was posted to III./JG 52, so that after almost two years at different schools and non-operational units, I was finally on my way to joint a front-line fighter unit. I had travelled as far as Düsseldorf, however, when I received a telegram informing me to report instead to Berlin-Döberitz. The III./JG 52 had suffered heavy losses during the fighting against Britain and was at Berlin-Döberitz recovering.

Once the *Gruppe* had been brought back to its established strength, it was transferred to Bucharest, in Rumania, where it was to protect the Ploesti oilfields. At the same time, we also trained Rumanian fighter pilots in the tactics employed in the *Luftwaffe* and, in recognition of this, I was presented on behalf of the King with the Rumanian pilots' badge.

When the Russian campaign began, things were quiet and we soon transferred to the southern part of the Eastern Front where III./JG 52 was to become very successful. In the beginning, the Russians were easy opponents as their biplanes were obsolete and their pilots often appeared frightened when they saw a German fighter approaching. But soon, MiG, Yak and LaGG fighters flown by well-motivated pilots began to appear and things gradually became more and more dangerous for us. They had very good aircraft, lighter than ours and easier to handle.

At this time the *Staffel* was split into two parts so that as soon as one part landed the other took off and continued operations. After a mission, the fuel tanks were replenished, the guns rearmed and the aircraft made ready to take-off again as soon as possible. Meanwhile, the pilots were able to grab a quick bite to eat and were supposed to have a short rest. In fact, our tents were not suitable places in which to really relax, probably unlike our opponents who were based on real airfields. Nevertheless, at least until the winter came, the food was quite good.

I claimed my first victory, an I-16, on 1 September 1941. My second *Abschuss*, another I-16, was also the 50th for 9./JG 52 and the 242nd for III./JG 52. Here is the official report:

*Victory over an I-16, 5 km N. of Charkow, 3 October, 1941, 17.02 Hours, Altitude: 1,500 m*

*On 3 October 1941, I flew as Rottenflieger to Lt. Graf on a low-level mission against an airfield north of Charkow, during which Lt. Graf was able to destroy two enemy aircraft on the ground. After the attack, we dived to 1,500 metres. North-west of Charkow, we spotted at an altitude of 2,000 metres a formation of about 20 Russian fighters of different types. I attacked the last, an I-16, from the rear and after a burst of gunfire it emitted heavy black smoke and fell almost vertically to the ground where it crashed. I was not able to observe the precise point of impact as I was myself attacked by several Russian aircraft, but it was witnessed by Lt. Graf.*

of VVS ChF's 32 IAP, equipped with Yak-1s. On 30 September, *Kapitan* Lyubimov and *St.Lt.* Mikhail Avdeyev, one of his best pilots, intercepted a pair of Bf 109s from 4./JG 77 and shot one down. The Bf 109's pilot, *Uffz.* Julius Dite, baled out and although he was taken prisoner, Dite later perished in captivity. However, his pistol, which he reportedly handed over to Lyubimov and Avdeyev, is today on display in St. Petersburg's Central Navy Museum.

On 1 October, III./JG 77 claimed three I-16s shot down but lost two Bf 109s. Two days later, LIV *Armee Korps* under the German 11th Army described the air situation at the Perekop Isthmus thus:

"The enemy air force was very active throughout the day, attacking villages, artillery positions and troop quarters in relentless waves (up to 27 aircraft participating in a single attack) to such an extent that [the situation] can only be described as [the enemy] having total control of the air."

A severe loss was inflicted on III./JG 77 on 8 October when 38-victory ace *Oblt.* Kurt Lasse, the *Staffelkapitän* of 9./JG 77, was killed during air combat with two MiG-3s. According to a German report, Lasse collided with his wingman, *Fw.* Robert Helmer.

Meanwhile, a new front was opened as German 1. *Panzergruppe* wheeled from the area east of Kiev and advanced south-eastwards to the Sea of Azov, enveloping the Soviet 18th and 9th Armies. On 9 October, VVS Southern Front, which was left with only 134 serviceable aircraft on 1 October, made strong

Uffz. Julius Dite's pistol as displayed today in the St. Petersburg Central Navy Museum.

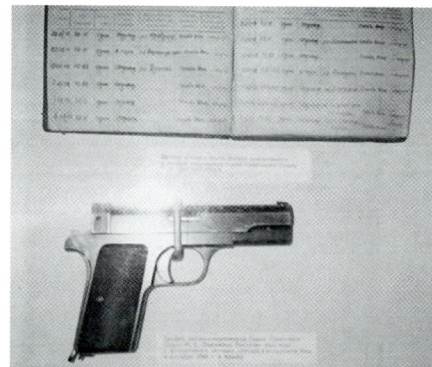

attempts to relieve the entrapped forces, but 4 ShAP and 210 ShAP, despatched to attack 1. *Panzergruppe*, were met by II./JG 77 which claimed eight Il-2s shot down during repeated clashes during the day. Other Soviet units suffered even worse during attacks on the German air base at Chaplinka, north of the Perekop Isthmus, and when the day was over, III./JG 77 had claimed 14 of the raiders, four being awarded to *Oblt*. Kurt Ubben who thus achieved his 45th victory.

Nevertheless, the pressure exerted by the VVS on 11th Army in the Perekop Isthmus could not be broken and *General* Erich von Manstein, commanding 11th Army, pointed out that even the German anti-aircraft batteries hesitated to open fire for fear of revealing their positions. To help resolve this situation, II./JG 3 was withdrawn from Operation *'Typhoon'*. This *Gruppe*, commanded by Knight's Cross holder *Hptm*. Gordon Gollob, was at that time one of the most successful *Jagdgruppen* and had been credited with more than 400 victories in the East since 22 June 1941. Arriving at Chaplinka on 16 October, II./JG 3 carried out its first mission over the Crimea the next day. This involved escorting bombers to Yevpatoria and during this mission, *Hptm*. Gollob claimed his 59th and 60th victories. Confident that Gollob's fighters would provide his troops with sufficient air cover, *General* von Manstein launched his next attack against the Crimea on 18 October. Gollob did what he could to break the Soviet air superiority, noting in his diary that day: *"Nine victories, all against I-16s* [actually MiG-3s]. *First take-off at 06.47 hrs: two victories; second take-off at 09.45 hrs: five victories; third take-off at 1430 hours: two victories."*

On the ground, German troops did indeed note a certain relief, but it was far from sufficient and, once again, the German attack broke down under the weight of Soviet air attacks, one of which, a surprise attack carried out the following night by Pe-2s of 40 BAP/VVS ChF, succeeded in neutralising Chaplinka aerodrome. Eventually, German fighter forces were further reinforced by the arrival of III./JG 52 and this proved to be the key to German victory in this sector. On 23 October, II./JG 3, III./JG 52 and III./JG 77, led by the inspector of the *Luftwaffe* fighter arm, *Oberst* Werner Mölders, then acting as *Nahkampfführer Krim*, were launched *en masse* against Soviet aircraft swarming over the Perekop Isthmus. By the end of the day, 34 Soviet aircraft had been claimed shot down, and 11th Army had achieved a decisive breakthrough. The next day, II./JG 3 and III./JG 52 dealt harshly with the weak Soviet fighter units that arrived on the scene and tried to regain what had been lost in the air on the 23rd. In III./JG 52, *Oblt*. Günther Rall shot down an I-153 and an I-16 for his 27th and 28th victories, *Lt*. Hermann Graf knocked down two "I-61s" for his 15th and 16th victories, and *Lt*. Adolf Dickfeld claimed five victories, bringing his total to 20. Meanwhile, *Hptm*. Gollob destroyed an I-153 for his 85th victory and on 26 October he was awarded the Oak Leaves to his Knight's Cross.

During the next few days 11th Army was able to occupy almost the entire Crimea, the exceptions being the Kerch peninsula, which was not cleared until May 1942, and the heavily fortified strategic port at Sevastopol which held out until July 1942. In early November, II./JG 3 left the Eastern Front and was transferred to Germany for a period of badly needed rest. Its aircraft were handed over to III./JG 77 which remained based in the Crimea, *Hptm*. Gollob's personal aircraft being taken over by *Oberst* Mölders, the *General der Jagdflieger*, who preferred to stay with III./JG 77 rather than to return to his office in Berlin. Albeit grounded on Hitler's orders, Mölders continued to fly unofficial combat missions with III./JG 77 in November 1941 and even achieved a number of unofficial aerial victories.

In November 1941, Oberst Werner Mölders was flying in action with III./JG 77 in the Sevastopol area of the Crimea. At that time, he was acting as a Nahkampf-führer, or Close-Support Leader, with command of fighter and ground-attack units. Despite Hitler's order forbidding him to fly on operations, on 8 November Mölders took off with Ofw. Herbert Kaiser for a mission over the front in which Mölders shot down an Il-2 which, naturally, he did not claim, and Kaiser shot down another two as his 23rd and 24th victories. Note that on this occasion, Mölders flew a Bf 109 F-4 which had previously belonged to the Stab II./JG 3

# June-December 1941

Oblt. Kurt Ubben, who had previously led 8./JG 77, was appointed Kommandeur of III./JG 77 on 5 September 1941, taking over from Major Alexander von Winterfeldt. Here, Ubben is seen returning from a sortie in his 'Black 13'.

**Messerschmitt Bf 109 F-4 flown by Oblt. Kurt Ubben, Kommandeur of III./JG 77, September 1941**
The camouflage finish on 'Black 13' evidently consisted of a heavy mottle of Green 70 sprayed over the original finish in such a way that the earlier 74/75 mottles on the fuselage showed through as darker areas. The finish was then further modified with lighter mottles of 02 and 74. Undersurfaces remained Light Blue 76 and yellow theatre markings were applied beneath the engine cowling, under the wingtips and around the fuselage. The latter band is unusual in being edged in red. The spinner was predominantly Green 70 with a red tip and the rudder is marked with 35 victory bars surmounted by a small representation of the Ritterkreuz complete with ribbon. The reason why the 20th victory bar, dated 25 July 1941, is in a different colour is not known.

*RIGHT*: Oblt. Ubben became very successful in Russia and by 25 July 1941 had already increased his score to 20 victories. He received the Ritterkreuz on 4 September with 28 victories and claimed his 36th victory, an I-16, on the day he became Kommandeur. In this photograph Ubben is standing on the right.

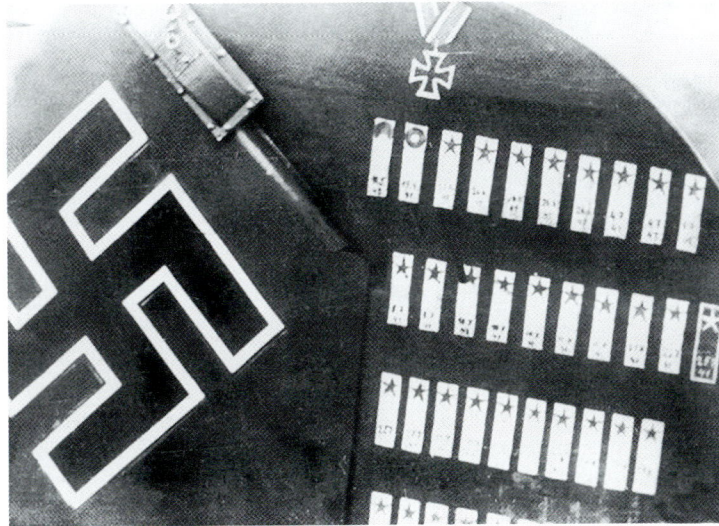

*RIGHT*: A closer view of the Knight's Cross emblem on Ubben's rudder which now shows a total of 39 victory bars. Ubben's first victory was a Dutch Fokker D-XXI fighter destroyed on 10 May 1940, and his second, an RAF Hurricane, on 19 April 1941. All the remaining victories were against Russian aircraft. Soon after the 39th victory bar had been added, Ubben's aircraft, still with the gust lock in place, was evidently captured by the Russians who photographed his rudder decoration.

*BELOW*: This Bf 109 F of Stab III./JG 77, photographed in the early Autumn of 1941, carried 30 victory bars on the rudder and, although the pilot has not been positively identified, it is believed that this is a reserve aircraft used by Oblt. Kurt Ubben.

*BELOW*: A portrait of Hptm. Kurt Ubben, taken after he had been awarded the Oak Leaves on 12 March 1942. After service in Russia, Kurt Ubben's III./JG 77 was transferred to North Africa and he later achieved his 100th victory in Tunisia. In March 1944 Ubben became Kommodore of JG 2 in the West but was killed in France on 27 April 1944. At the time of his death he had been credited with a total of 110 victories.

# June-December 1941

In early September, Lt. Otto Schlosser of 4./JG 53 was apparently involved in two accidents. On the first occasion, Schlosser is believed to have stalled while landing, with the result shown here. A few days later, on 6 September, II./JG 53 moved to Lyuban, 66 km south of Schlisselburg in Northern Russia, in order to support army operations in that area. During the first day's operations from the new airfield, Schlosser was killed when his Bf 109 F-4, W.Nr. 8389, struck an obstacle while taking off.

*LEFT*: It was not uncommon for Luftwaffe units in the East to be based on any convenient piece of land which was flat and free of large stones, the most suitable frequently being cultivated areas. Consequently, flying units often found themselves operating close to farm workers tending their crops and frequently shared the same field. Despite the obvious dangers of working on a busy airfield, the relationship between the local inhabitants and Germans was beneficial, German chocolate or tinned rations being exchanged for eggs and fresh fruit and vegetables.

*RIGHT AND BELOW*: On 23 October 1941, Uffz. Alfred Grislawski took off in this Bf 109 F-4 from Poltava aerodrome. After only a few minutes' flight, the engine seized and Grislawski had to make a rapid forced landing, during the course of which one wing of his aircraft struck a Russian woman working in the fields. Grislawski attended to her injuries and she was later taken to hospital in a German army lorry. Grislawski had first joined III./JG 52 in August 1940 and served in 7. Staffel before transferring to 9. Staffel. A large number of his operational sorties were flown as wingman to Hermann Graf who, in 1942, became the first pilot to reach 200 victories. Grislawski himself also became one of the most successful fighter pilots of the war, reaching a total of 132 victories. After the war, Grislawski refused an offer to join the Bundesluftwaffe and, at the time of writing, is still alive.

**Messerschmitt Bf 109 F-4 'Yellow 8' flown by Uffz. Alfred Grislawski of 9./JG 52**
Showing a modified camouflage of Green 70 over the original grey scheme, this aircraft typifies the appearance of 9./JG 52's aircraft during the early months of the Russian campaign. Of interest is the use of different shades of yellow, the theatre markings and aircraft identification being noticeably darker than the spinner and fuselage band. Note also the Green 70 spinner backplate.

III./JG 52 badge

## In the Far North

On the extreme north flank of Germany's war against the Soviet Union, *Wehrmacht* forces marched from German-occupied northern Norway to seize the town of Murmansk, the Soviet Union's only port which remained ice-free throughout the year and had direct access to the open seas. At the outbreak of hostilities, the operation against Murmansk was supported by *Luftwaffenkommando Kirkenes*, a detachment from *Luftflotte* 5 which mustered some 100 aircraft including about 20 Bf 109 Es from 1. and 14./JG 77. This force was opposed by 263 Soviet aircraft, none of which included the most modern types.

In contrast to the other sectors of the Eastern Front, there was almost no flying on 22 June 1941 due to thick fog and one of the *Luftwaffe's* first operations in the Far North was carried out on a later date when a *Rotte* composed of *Oblt.* Horst Carganico, *Staffelkapitän* of 1./JG 77, and *Ofw.* Hugo Dahmer, strafed the large Soviet lighthouse at the mouth of Kola Bay, the entrance to Murmansk. The two *Jagdwaffe* pilots were later strongly rebuked for this action, since German U-boats operating in this area used the lighthouse as an orientation point.

Carganico and Dahmer would soon earn fame as the deadliest *Luftwaffe* duo in the Far North. When the war against the USSR opened, Carganico had six victories, whereas Dahmer's score already stood at 11, reached while serving with JG 26 in the West. In fact, Dahmer, who had better eyesight than Carganico, also developed the so-called *Sauhaufen*, or "hog wild" tactics, that led him and his *Staffelkapitän* to great success. According to these tactics, Carganico and Dahmer attacked Soviet bomber formations singly, relentlessly and irregularly, each from various directions, confusing the Soviet bombers' gunners by creating the impression that there were more than two German fighters attacking.

The progress of *Luftwaffe* operations in the Far North was assisted when Finland joined the war on Germany's side and, after a while, a *Freya* early warning radar was installed to support *Luftwaffenkommando Kirkenes*. This was quite unique, being the only case on the Eastern Front in 1941 when the *Luftwaffe* could make any use of radar, but despite this technical advantage the airmen had to fight hard. There were several highly experienced Soviet pilots serving in this sector, and one of them, *St.Lt.* Boris Safonov of the Northern Fleet's (SF) 72 SAP, would develop into the most successful Soviet fighter ace of 1941. Although *Hptm.* Alfred von Lojewski, *Staffelkapitän* of 14./JG 77, was shot down on 29 June and was captured, on most occasions the German fighters had the upper hand against the Soviet Polikarpov fighters and SB bombers.

By 12 July, Dahmer's victory tally had reached 22 while *Oblt.* Carganico's stood at 13. At this time, Carganico and Dahmer were stationed at Petsamo, the Finnish town that had been annexed by the Soviets in 1940, and when the German Army's advance against Murmansk failed and both sides became bogged down in static warfare, wild dogfights took place in the air over the frontline. This was the period of the Polar Summer, when the sun shone for 24 hours and rendered air operations possible around the clock. *Oblt.* Carganico achieved an unusual victory on 25 July when he shot down an MBR-2 seaplane, but his air combat five days later would be even more spectacular. At this time the British aircraft carriers HMS *Victorious* and *Furious* were operating in northern waters, and on 30 July, 30 Fairey Albacore torpedo aircraft and nine Fairey Fulmar fighters from the Royal Navy's 827, 828 and 817 Squadrons, took off from these vessels to attack German ships at Kirkenes. The British formations were intercepted by nine Bf 109s from *Hptm.* Carganico's 1./JG 77 and four Bf 110s from the neighbouring 1.(Z)/JG 77. A total of 12 Albacores and four Fulmars were shot down (the Germans claimed 28) for the loss of a Bf 110 and a Ju 87. Although *Ofw.* Dahmer did not participate in this action, two days later he achieved his 25th victory against a Soviet aircraft and became the first pilot in the Far North to be awarded the Knight's Cross.

Another successful pilot in 1./JG 77 was *Lt.* Heinz Mahlkuch, who had a total of 16 victories before being posted missing in action on 23 August 1941. Shortly afterward, a 20 year-old *Unteroffizier* was posted to 1./JG 77 from the *Ergänzungsgruppe*. His name was Rudolf Müller, and on only his third combat flight, on 12 September 1941, he scored his first victory against an I-16 followed by a DB-3 and an I-153 on 17 September. Müller would eventually become one of the highest scoring *Luftwaffe* pilots in the Far North.

Oblt. Horst Carganico who, at the beginning of 'Barbarossa', was Staffelkapitän of 1./JG 77. This photograph shows Carganico after he had been awarded the Ritterkreuz on 25 September 1941.

Ofw. Hugo Dahmer, who with Carganico, developed a particularly successful method of attacking Soviet bomber formations.

By this time Soviet air forces in the Far North were being reinforced. MiG-3s and LaGG-3s arrived to replace the Polikarpov fighters, and Western lend-lease war equipment started arriving by sea aboard convoys sailing into Murmansk. The first convoy brought the RAF's 81 and 134 Squadrons with a total of 39 Hurricane fighters, and the British pilots carried out their first combat in this sector on 12 September when a Bf 109 E was shot down for the loss of a Hurricane. However, contrary to various British accounts, the Hurricanes, whether flown by British or Soviet pilots, did not bring any decisive qualitative improvement to the Soviet side, and of the three Bf 109s claimed shot down by the British Hurricane pilots on 26 September, for example, not one can be confirmed by German loss records. In contrast, however, the new pilot *Uffz.* Rudolf Müller shot down one of these Hurricanes on the 27th as his fourth victory.

During the first three months of operations against the Soviets, 1./JG 77 was credited with about 100 victories for the loss of 10 Bf 109s and three pilots. On 25 September, two days before his 24th birthday, *Oblt.* Carganico became the *Staffel's* second Knight's Cross holder with a victory tally of 27. By that time, the *Jagdstaffeln* in the Far North had been united under the command of *Major* Hennig Strümpell to form the *Jagdgruppe zur besonderen Verwendung,* or Fighter Group for Special Duties.

From October 1941 the approaching Polar winter with its greatly reduced hours of daylight and adverse weather severely curtailed flying in the Far North. A *Schwarm* commanded by Dahmer was transferred to an airfield near Alakurtti, 175 miles south-west of Murmansk, to support the Finnish III. Army Corps' attack in this area. On 25 October, Dahmer's *Schwarm* took off to attack a Soviet army patrol of about 150–200 men which had penetrated the Finnish lines during the night and had surrounded Alakurtti aerodrome. During two strafing missions, the four Bf 109s managed to almost completely wipe out the Soviet unit.

*Uffz.* Müller shot down his next Soviet aircraft, two SBs and an I-16, on 2 and 4 November, and a few days later, 1./JG 77 was withdrawn from first-line service. During the last weeks of 1941, it became apparent even from the relatively few encounters in the air, that Soviet aerial opposition had improved. When *Lt.* Alfred Jakobi of *Jagdgruppe z.b.V.* was shot down and wounded in his shoulder by a Soviet Hurricane near Zapadnaya Litsa, his aircraft became number 15 on Boris Safonov's list of shot-down German aircraft; 20 if Safonov's shared victories are included.

A troublesome incident took place on 8 November, when the newly appointed *Jagdfliegerführer Norwegen, Oberst* Carl Schumacher, flying a mission in a Bf 109, misidentified a Finnish De Havilland Dragon Rapide ambulance aircraft. Believing it was a Soviet SB bomber, Schumacher attacked and shot down the Finnish aircraft. Fortunately, there were no fatalities, and to avoid an awkward incident, the Germans awarded the Finnish crew with Iron Crosses and rapidly transferred Schumacher to another position.

A comparison between German and Soviet loss files show that whereas *Luftflotte* 5 registered 89 aircraft destroyed or severely damaged due to enemy action in the air between June and November 1941, the Soviets lost 221 aircraft in combat with both *Luftflotte* 5 and the Finnish Air Force.

## Failure

In late October and early November 1941, the notorious Russian *rasputitsa* – the deep mud created by the heavy autumnal rainfall – almost brought the German offensive along the entire Eastern Front to a complete standstill. The VVS tried to exploit this situation by attacking the columns of stranded German vehicles, and whenever conditions permitted, the Bf 109s of the *Jagdgeschwader* in the East carried out *freie Jagd* standing patrols over the front area. On the Northern Front, JG 54 reported eleven kills on 6 November, thus bringing the *Geschwader's* total number of victories to over 1,500, and to the south, over the road to Rostov, I. (*J*)/LG 2, III./JG 52 and II./JG 77 dealt the VVS airmen grievous losses. Of these *Jagdgruppen,* III./JG 52, which had transferred to Taganrog on the northern shore of the Sea of Azov on 2 November, was particularly successful. *Fw.* Gerhard Köppen achieved the *Gruppe's* 400th victory in early November, the *Staffelkapitän* of 8./JG 52, *Oblt.* Rall, achieved his 30th victory

An SdKfz 7 8-ton half-track vehicle towing a Bf 109 F of 2./JG 54 through the mud at Lissino airfield in the early Autumn of 1941.

when he shot down a MiG-3 on 8 November, and throughout the month the *Gruppe's* victory-to-loss ratio was 20:1.

The most effective resistance in the air was encountered by *Luftflotte* 2 near Moscow where the Soviets gave the defence of the city the highest priority and, indeed, the proportion of modern Soviet aircraft was larger here than anywhere else along the front. Nor was the situation helped when the whole of II. *Fliegerkorps* left *Luftflotte* 2 and transferred to the Mediterranean where it was required to attack Malta, the British base which threatened German convoys to North Africa. After the departure of the last elements of JG 3, JG 27 and JG 53, the only *Jagdwaffe* units left to provide Army Group Centre with air cover were JG 51 and I. and II./JG 52. During November, JG 51 registered an average of ten victories for every loss and on 4 November recorded 18 Soviet aircraft shot down against two losses. Between the 4th and 15th, I./JG 52 achieved 35 victories against four losses, but included among its casualties was the *Gruppenkommandeur*, *Oblt.* Karl-Heinz Leesmann, who was seriously injured in air combat on the 6th; Leesmann had 32 victories and had been awarded the Knight's Cross. On 13 November, the 57-victory ace *Ofw.* Edmund Wagner of 9./JG 51 had just shot down a Pe-2 bomber when his Bf 109 F-2, 'Yellow 1', was hit by defensive fire from a Soviet bomber and crashed near Pafmutovka.

With the arrival of the Russian winter in mid-November, the roads froze and the German advance could be resumed, 1. *Panzer* Army renewing its offensive against Rostov on 17 November. Here the Soviets tried to block the advance by launching heavy air strikes and, on 17 November alone, the VVS carried out a total of 400 sorties but was stalled by III./JG 52 and II./JG 77. That day, 9./JG 52's *Staffelführer, Lt.* Hermann Graf, achieved his 25th victory by shooting down an I-16. When the first German troops reached Rostov on 20 November, III./JG 52 still had 18 serviceable Bf 109s to hand and was in firm control of the air in this sector.

Nevertheless, the *Wehrmacht* was inevitably losing its strength as battle fatigue, over-extended supply lines and a chronic lack of spares and replacements made it increasingly difficult to fulfil demands. Indeed, it was largely due to the deteriorating supply situation in the East that Ernst Udet, the *Luftwaffe's* chief of supply and procurement, was driven to commit suicide on 17 November. Five days later, the *General der Jagdflieger, Oberst* Werner Mölders, boarded an He 111 of KG 27 at Chaplinka in order to fly to Udet's state funeral, but the Heinkel crashed in bad weather during an intermediate stop at Breslau, killing the popular fighter leader. To preserve his memory, JG 51 was awarded the honour-title *Jagdgeschwader Mölders* on 24 November and, similarly, the honour-title *Jagdgeschwader Udet* was later bestowed upon JG 3.

On 27 November, a sharp drop in temperature added to the Germans' problems and in the Moscow area a temperature was measured of –40°C The *Wehrmacht* was totally ill-prepared to meet such harsh conditions and found itself with troops that lacked suitable clothing and had technical equipment not designed to operate at such low temperatures. The *Luftwaffe,* too, was frequently paralysed by the cold as most first-line units were based largely on primitive front airstrips where there were no heated hangars available.

Conversely, the Red Army and VVS proved far better prepared to meet such harsh conditions and on 28 November incessant Soviet air attacks succeeded in halting the 10th Motorised Division of Guderian's 2. *Panzer* Army. Only a few of JG 51's Bf 109s could take off that day, and although they shot down a total of five Soviet aircraft, this was hardly sufficient to block the Soviet air attacks. Also on 28 November, 8./JG 52's *Oblt.* Günther Rall was severely injured when his Bf 109 F-4 was shot down by a Yak-1 near Rostov. Two days later, a Soviet flank attack against the 1. *Panzer* Army succeeded in forcing the Germans to withdraw from Rostov.

On 2 December, a clear day with temperatures of around –15°C, Army Group Centre made a final effort to seize Moscow and actually managed to penetrate the Moscow suburb of Khimki before its forces were halted by tenacious Soviet resistance. On account of the favourable weather, both *Luftflotte* 2 and the VVS could send all available forces to support the ground fighting and JG 51 claimed a total of 18 Soviet aircraft destroyed, the *Gruppenkommandeur* of II./JG 51, *Hptm.* Hartmann Grasser, achieving his 40th victory while the *Staffelkapitän* of 4./JG 52, *Oblt.* Johannes Steinhoff, claimed his 50th.

Ofw. Edmund Wagner of 9./JG 51 claimed his first victory over England on 14 September 1940 and had no more victories until 24 June 1941 when he shot down four Russian bombers. Here, Obstlt. Werner Mölders congratulates Wagner on his achievement. Subsequently, Wagner's victory tally increased dramatically, and by 28 October his total had reached 50. However, Wagner's career was short and on 13 November, by which time his score had risen to 57, he was killed in action. He was awarded a posthumous Ritterkreuz four days later.

Oblt. Karl-Heinz Leesmann, the Kommandeur of I./JG 52, claimed 10 victories in Russia within about a month before being wounded during an air battle over Klin, 90 km NW of Moscow, on 6 November 1941. As a result of his injuries, Leesmann had to leave his Gruppe until he had partially recovered and, although he returned to the front and resumed command in May 1942, he led his unit from the ground.

LEFT: On 22 November, Oberst Werner Mölders boarded a Heinkel 111 of KG 27 at Chaplinka which was to fly him back to Germany where he was to attend the funeral of the Luftwaffe's chief of procurement and supply, Ernst Udet. However, the aircraft in which he was a passenger crashed at Breslau-Gandau and Mölders was killed.

**28. 11. 41.**

**Staatsbegräbnis Oberst Mölders**

**Wagenkarte**

Bitte an Windschutzscheibe befestigen! Bitte Rückseite beachten!

ABOVE: A parking permit for mourners at Mölders' Staatsbegräbnis, or state funeral. The ceremony was attended by Göring (LEFT), seen here walking behind the gun-carriage bearing Mölders's coffin.

RIGHT: The Führer pays his respects.

BELOW: Reichsmarschall Göring leading the funeral procession. In the front rank, from left to right, are Siegfried Schnell, Josef Priller, Hans 'Assi' Hahn and Werner Streib. Erhard Milch is visible between Schnell and Priller.

BELOW RIGHT: The Reichsmarschall raises his baton in a final salute to Mölders whose death was a severe blow for the Wehrmacht, and especially for JG 51. Later, this unit was awarded an honour-title and officers and men serving with the Geschwader were entitled to wear on their right sleeve a cuff band embroidered with the words "Jagdgeschwader Mölders".

# June-December 1941

Despite these successes, however, *Luftflotte* 2 was gradually losing the battle for air superiority in the skies above Army Group Centre and by 6 December, when the Soviets counter-attacked in the Moscow area, it could commit less than 600 aircraft against the Soviets' 1,376. During the first days of the Soviet counter-offensive, air operations were complicated by a low-pressure system which brought mild air to the Moscow area and created a thick fog. As the German ground troops fell back in increasing disorder, the German fighters flew low-level ground-strafing sorties against the Soviet advance columns and, as a result, JG 51 achieved no more than a dozen victories between 6 and 10 December.

To the north of Moscow, with clear skies and sinking temperatures, the Soviets retook Tikhvin on 9 December and, on 13 December, the VVS Kalinin Front carried out a devastating raid against Klin aerodrome north-west of Moscow, knocking out half of II./JG 52's aircraft park before the airfield was evacuated due to the Soviet advance. *Luftwaffe* statistics show that between 13 and 19 December, the amount of air activity declined sharply and that in this period only 45 aerial victories were claimed along the entire Eastern Front. Aided by reinforcements, a greatly strengthened *Luftflotte* 2 then ordered all available aircraft against the advancing Soviet troops and helped Army Group Centre to bring the Soviet offensive to a halt during the last week of the year. But by that time, German forces all along the Eastern Front had been forced onto the defensive.

On 28 November, Oblt. Günther Rall, the Staffelkapitän of 8./JG 52, was involved in an air battle in which he was wounded and his Bf 109 F-4, 'Black 1', W.Nr. 7308, crash-landed near Rostov. Although appearing relatively intact in this photograph, the airframe probably suffered severe structural damage as it was later classified as 95% destroyed and written off.

*ABOVE AND RIGHT*: With the beginning of bad weather on the Eastern Front, the temperature dropped to as low as -45°C. These Bf 109 F-4s of III./JG 52 belonged to 8. Staffel (*ABOVE*) and 9. Staffel (*RIGHT*).

June-December 1941

*ABOVE*: A flight of Bf 109 F-2s from JG 51 in the Winter of 1941/42.

*BELOW*: On 15 November, Lt. Hans Hopp, who had a single victory, and also Lt.Walter Schick, both of 2./JG 51, were posted missing.At the time, Hopp was flying 'Black 2' and Schick, who had ten victories, an F-2, W.Nr. 9713, coded 'Black 5'. This photograph is believed to show Walter Schick's aircraft after it was later discovered by German ground troops.There was, however, no trace of the pilot.

*BELOW*: These snow-camouflaged Bf 109 F-2s are believed to have belonged to II./JG 51 which arrived at Bryansk on 30 December 1941. Note that while the upper nose cowling on the aircraft to the right has been painted white, the two other machines have retained completely yellow cowlings.

*LEFT AND BELOW:* Members of I./JG 51 with a Bf 109 F-2 in the Winter of 1941/42. The pilot on the left in both photographs is believed to be Oblt. Heinrich Krafft, Staffelkapitän of 3./JG 51 since 11 November 1940. Nicknamed "Gaudi", or "Fun", on account of his sense of humour, he claimed four victories during the Western campaign before being seriously wounded in May 1940. He returned to his unit in June 1941 and, on the opening day of 'Barbarossa', when he made his first war flight since being wounded, claimed four victories. By the end of 1941, Krafft had 34 Luftsiegen.

*RIGHT:* In the Northern Sector, JG 54 carried out fighter-bomber attacks against such targets as airfields, tanks, lorries, sleds, columns, troop concentrations and railway trains. It was found that although railway stations were frequently crowded with trains, anti-aircraft protection was especially strong and that effective attacks could not be carried out. Operations were therefore flown against moving trains which were between stations and the disruption of the Soviet's supplies proved so effective that they were forced to provide fighter protection over all major railway lines. 500kg bombs were not dropped during the winter months and this Bf 109 F fighter-bomber has been loaded with a 250 kg weapon which was usually employed when attacking towns, bridges, and other buildings of rigid construction. Returning with bombs still attached was not permitted due to the risks associated with overstraining the undercarriage.

June-December 1941

*BELOW*: The rudder of Lt. Heinz Lange's Bf 109 F-2, 'Black 5', of 8./JG 54, photographed at Dünaburg after Lange's fifth victory. On 1 October 1941, Lange became Staffelkapitän of 1./JG 54, taking over from Reinhard Seiler who became Kommandeur of III. Gruppe. Lange was awarded the Ritterkreuz on 18 November 1941 and ended the war with 70 victories. The aircraft shown here was 50% damaged on 6 July 1941.

*ABOVE*: A German soldier posing with a Bf 109 F-2 coded 'Black 3' of 8./JG 54 which crash-landed in October or November 1941.
Note the armoured windscreen and the variety of different colours on the propeller spinner.

*BELOW*: Three pilots of Erg. Gr. JG 54 in the Autumn of 1941. On the far left is Uffz. Karl "Quax" Schnörrer who, soon after this photograph was taken, was posted to 1./JG 54. He claimed his first victory on 13 December and was greatly appreciated by the aces of his Gruppe who considered him an excellent Kaczmarek who, at the expense of his own claims, always placed himself at his leader's disposal. Nevertheless, he eventually claimed a final tally of 46 victories, was awarded the Ritterkreuz in March 1945, and survived the war. The aircraft in the background carries the emblem of Erg. JG 54 on the cowling.

# June-December 1941

*ABOVE*: Two snow-camouflaged aircraft of the Stab/JG 54 at Relbitsy in Northern Russia. The machine on the right was flown by the Kommodore, Major Hannes Trautloft, and had green Stab markings outlined in black. The aircraft on the left, with similar camouflage and markings, is the subject of our profile and was flown by Oblt. Otto Kath who had previously served with Trautloft in III./JG 51. In August 1940, when Trautloft left to take command of JG 54, he was permitted by Jagdfliegerführer General von Döring, to take several of his friends with him. These included his First Mechanic, Obgfr. Pingel, his driver, Obgfr. Books, his wingman Uffz. Deutschmann, as well as Oblt. Werner Pichon-Kalau von Hofe and his adjutant, Oblt. Kath.

*LEFT*: Another view of Kath's machine in the Winter of 1941/42, at which time he had six victories, the latest being achieved early in the Russian campaign on 24 July 1941.

**JG 54 'Grünherz' emblem**

## Messerschmitt Bf 109 F-4 flown by Oblt. Otto Kath, Stab/JG 54

With a temporary winter finish applied over its original camouflage colours, this aircraft clearly shows the effects of weathering on such a scheme. In this case, however, the finish has not yet worn off and apart from normal wear and tear, has become further soiled by the heavy black carbon deposit emanating from the exhausts. Six victory bars appear on the yellow rudder and traces of the original Green 71 spinner and its white segment may be seen through the temporary white winter finish. Note that no attempt has been made to repaint the canopy frames. Lt. Kath flew as wingman to the Geschwaderkommodore, Hannes Trautloft.

# June-December 1941

*RIGHT*: A Bf 109 F of Erg./JG 54 in November 1941. Note the unit emblem on the nose and the warm winter clothing worn by the ground personnel.

## Messerschmitt Bf 109 F-4 'Black 16' of JG 54
The contrast between the white camouflage on this machine and the exposed areas beneath suggests this machine was camouflaged in the colours 70 and 71 before receiving the white winter finish. Undersurfaces are Grey 76. As seen on a number of JG 54's aircraft operating in winter conditions, the oleo fairings have been removed from the undercarriage.

*LEFT*: Apart from its canopy framing, this Bf 109 F-4 of JG 54 has been painted in a temporary white finish for operations in the Winter of 1941/42 and is seen here displaying some wear. In particular, the white area under the cockpit has worn away to reveal part of the JG 54 'Greenheart' emblem and the lower rudder, always an area to receive severe buffeting from the slipstream and erosion from loose snow, ice or other debris, shows similar signs of wear.

# June-December 1941

*ABOVE*: Weapons personnel with a Bf 109 E fighter-bomber in Russia. Even on snow-covered airfields, no difficulties were encountered in taxiing or taking off with bomb-laden aircraft, provided the maximum bomb load did not exceed 250 kg, that the surface of the runway had been hardened by rolling, and the aircraft was taxied at high speed. Extremely rapid turns had to be avoided, however, as this caused the outside wheel to press into the snow. A particular problem which arose in the Winter of 1941/42 when targets immediately ahead of friendly troops were attacked was that the winter clothing worn by both German and Russian forces made the identification of friendly and enemy troops extremely difficult. Because of this, there were several incidents when friendly troops were attacked in error and the soldiers' confidence in the Luftwaffe undermined. In this photograph, the Bf 109 F fighter in the background is believed to have the 'Gemsbock' emblem of I./JG 51, perhaps indicating that the fighter-bomber also belonged to JG 51.

*RIGHT*: Special protection in the form of heated shacks was erected by Luftwaffe ground staff around aircraft parked in the open. Known as 'Alert Boxes', these temporary structures prevented engines from freezing and allowed mechanics to continue servicing machines in low temperatures. This Bf 109 F is 'Yellow 1' of JG 51 in the winter of 1941/42.

June-December 1941

Bf 109 F flown by Fw. Rudolf Nielinger whose first operational posting was to 4./JG 51 at Mardijck on 29 March 1941. At that time the Staffel was equipped with Bf 109 Es and between 22 April and 1 June 1941 Nielinger flew several missions against England. He was then assigned a brand new Bf 109 F-2 and transferred to the East, flying his first combat mission of the Russian campaign from Liedice on 22 June, during which he was engaged in combat with three Soviet fighters over Brest-Litovsk. Nielinger gained his first victory on 25 June when, flying 'Yellow 6', he shot down an SB bomber. His second victory came on 3 July when, flying 'White 4', the aircraft shown here, he destroyed a DB-3. By the time 4./JG 51 transferred to North Africa in early September 1942, Neilinger was credited with 16 confirmed kills.

**Messerschmitt Bf 109 F-2 flown by Fw. Rudolf Nielinger of 4./JG 51**
An example of the temporary white finish applied over all aircraft uppersurfaces as a winter camouflage scheme. It was not until the attack on Russia that there was any requirement for a winter camouflage and, as the RLM had not anticipated such a requirement, the only suitable material available was a white, artificial resin emulsion paste known as Ikarin-A2515.21. This had originally been supplied to the German army as a means of applying a temporary winter finish and could be diluted and applied by brush or spray.

JG 51 'Mölders' badge

# June-December 1941

*ABOVE LEFT AND RIGHT*: The Bücker Bü 131 Jungmann was designed as a sports, aerobatics and training aircraft and first entered service with the Luftwaffe in 1935. This example, coded KG+GB, served with 2./JG 54 in late 1941 and although at least one source states that it later became a personal courier aircraft used by Oblt. Hans Phillip, who became the Kommandeur of I./JG 54 on 15 February 1942, the display of Abschussbalken on the rudder is believed to represent 2. Staffel's tally rather than Oblt. Phillip's own victories. The machine has received an overspray of white and the name "Lilli-Marlen" appears on the fuselage.

### Bücker Bü 131 "Jungmann" of I./JG 54

As appropriate for its original training role, this aircraft was originally painted in Light Grey L40/52 overall. Later, perhaps when first assigned to JG 54 as a liaison aircraft, it was repainted in a standard Green 70/71 uppersurface scheme with Blue 65 undersurfaces. At this time, the swastika was masked off, leaving a surrounding square of the original L40/52. Because of the more complicated masking involved, it would seem the fuselage cross and code letters were overpainted during respraying and, when reapplied, were incorrectly positioned, being higher than normal and not parallel with the aircraft centreline. Later, the uppersurfaces were again repainted with a temporary white snow camouflage which was applied unevenly and left areas of the green scheme showing through. This time, while the major part of the airframe was spray-painted, the white areas around the code letters were brushed on, leaving a green border which resulted in the slightly distorted appearance of the lettering. The name "Lilli-Marlen" (as opposed to the famous, and still popular, wartime song 'Lili Marlene') appeared in red under the cockpits, and the badge of 2./JG 54 on a white disc was painted on the yellow engine cowling.

*LEFT*: When photographed again in early 1942, the yellow cowling had been overpainted white and the badge of I./JG 54 had been added to its fuselage. This machine, one of at least two Bücker 131s operated by JG 54, is known to have survived until 1943.

# June-December 1941

Other communications and courier aircraft used on the Eastern Front included the Fieseler Fi 156 Storch and the Messerschmitt Bf 108. This Storch of III./JG 54 (*ABOVE*) seen in the Summer of 1941 is marked with the Geschwader and Gruppe emblems while, by way of contrast, the Bf 108 of JG 77 (*LEFT*) carries no unit identity but has been camouflaged in a suitable winter scheme.

# June-December 1941

*BELOW:* A black fuselage number and a horizontal bar, as in this winter scene of a Bf 109 F shrouded against the elements, normally indicate a machine of the 5. Staffel of a Jagdgeschwader, although which one is not known.

*LEFT AND BELOW:* Photographed during the Winter of 1941/42, 'Yellow 6' and 'Yellow 11' (*LEFT*) both belonged to 3./JG 54. Free use of the spray gun has been employed to apply a winter camouflage consisting of a tight pattern of almost continuous meandering lines. (*BELOW*) Technical and armament ground staff of 3./JG 54 at work on one of the Staffel's machines. This aircraft has a more solid application of white winter camouflage and the one-third white segment on the spinner is typical for the period, sometimes appearing with a sharp, obviously masked-off demarcation line, as seen here, while in other factories it was sprayed freehand resulting in a soft, feathered edge.

*RIGHT*: The modified scheme of 70 and 71 uppersurfaces over 76 undersurfaces on this Bf 109 F of 7./JG 54 has been overpainted with a white temporary finish for winter camouflage.

**Messerschmitt Bf 109 F of 7./JG 54**

This aircraft has been camouflaged in a winter scheme showing signs of considerable wear and weathering. Although the yellow nose had once also received a covering of white, this has largely worn off. Note that the oleo fairings have been removed from the undercarriage.

# June-December 1941

## Summary

The importance of the role played by the *Jagdwaffe* during Operation *'Barbarossa'* cannot be underestimated, for whenever the Bf 109s appeared in any strength they dominated the skies, often even when vastly outnumbered. In their first six months on the Eastern Front between June and December 1941, the *Jagdflieger* achieved previously unparalleled numerical successes and claimed a total of more than 7,000 aerial victories, a number which accords with Soviet loss statistics. These high Soviet losses were due to a combination of factors but mainly to the purging of the Red Army in the late 1930s and the *Luftwaffe's* superiority in combat experience, tactics and equipment. The most successful *Jagdgeschwader* during Operation *'Barbarossa'* was JG 51, which accounted for 1,820 victories in the East in 1941 against 240 of its aircraft destroyed or severely damaged. In the same period, JG 54 reported 1,185 victories against slightly more than 200 of its own aircraft destroyed or severely damaged.

Between 22 June and 6 December 1941, total *Luftwaffe* aircraft losses including aircraft damaged on the Eastern Front are recorded at 3,422, of which 2,093 were completely destroyed or written off. Total fighter losses amounted to 981, of which 568 were completely destroyed or written off. Compared with the number of Soviet aircraft destroyed, these German losses are surprisingly low but cannot be regarded as insignificant because of the inadequate supply system which made losses, however small, difficult to replace. For this reason, the attrition sustained by the *Luftwaffe* in the East in 1941 is one of the main reasons for the *Wehrmacht's* failure at the gates of Moscow in December.

## II.(Schlacht)/Lehrgeschwader 2

After action in the Balkans, II.(*Schlacht*)/LG 2 prepared for action in the East and provided valuable support for the ground forces. As with I.(*Jagd*) *Gruppe*, II. *Gruppe* was still equipped with the Bf 109 E and was in action from the first day of 'Barbarossa'. Its activities are summarised below.

| | |
|---|---|
| **22-24 June** | Supported the breakthrough of 9. Army and 3. *Panzergruppe* from the border fortifications east and south-east of Suwalki in East Prussia. |
| **25 June-1 July** | Took part in the encircling battles of Grodno, Bialystok and Minsk and participated in the advance of 3. *Panzergruppe* via Vitebsk to Smolensk. |
| **2-20 July** | Supported 2. *Panzergruppe* in the Dnieper River crossing. |
| **21-29 July** | In action against Russian forces defending Smolensk and took part in the battle of encirclement at Smolensk. |
| **7-26 August** | In support of 16. Army in drive to reach Novgorod. |
| **27 August-8 September** | Advanced with *Panzergruppe* Schmidt on Schlüsselburg. |
| **9-28 September** | Operated in support of 4. *Panzergruppe* in the attack on Leningrad and fought Russian counter-attacks near Lake Ladoga. |
| **2-7 October** | Participated in the battle of encirclement at Vyazma. |
| **8-14 October** | Supported the push on Kalinin with 3. *Panzergruppe* and AOK 9. |
| **28 October-28 November** | Took part in the battles to isolate Moscow from Tula to the south and from Klin to the north of the city. |
| **29 November** | Returned to home base in Germany for refitting. Later redesignated and formed part of *Schlachtgeschwader* 1, returning to the front in May 1942. |

*ABOVE*: Believed taken during the Russian campaign, this photograph shows 'Yellow E' of II.(Schlacht)/LG 2 taking off. Unfortunately, the badge on the fuselage side cannot be identified and no details are available date or precise location.

*LEFT*: Photographed early in the campaign in the East, 'Yellow C' of II.(Schlacht)/LG 2 stands on an airfield in the East with the wreckage of a Soviet aircraft in the foreground.

**June-December 1941**

In an endeavour to ensure all Jagdgeschwadern operating in Russia were kept adequately supplied with aircraft, a large infrastructure was necessary in the rear areas and several ferry units were required to fly aircraft up to the front. Even so, such was the extent of battle attrition that several Staffeln soon had only a few machines ready for operations. New aircraft still carrying factory codes were often ferried to Varsovya where they were collected by operational pilots who then flew them on to their front-line units. These photographs, all taken in Poland, show that theatre markings were sometimes applied at the factories and not always by the operational units themselves. In this connection, note however that while the aircraft seen (*LEFT*) has yellow under the wingtips and a yellow cowling, the latter is in two different shades suggesting that, contrary to then current regulations, the area of yellow originally applied only under the cowling, as seen on SG+YW (*BELOW LEFT*), was later enlarged to include the whole cowling. This variation in the yellow is seen more clearly in the view (*BELOW RIGHT*) showing SJ+MR in flight over Poland where the yellow of the fuselage band is noticeably darker than the yellow cowling. The remaining photographs show 'Yellow 11' and 'Yellow 5' presumably in transit back to their unit in Russia after being repaired or overhauled. 'Yellow 11' has 15 victory bars painted on its yellow rudder but the unit to which it belonged has, unfortunately, not been identified. Another view of 'Yellow 11' (*BOTTOM*) shows the aircraft was particularly clean and had a glossy spinner.

# June–December 1941

*BELOW*: This Bf 109 F, photographed in the late Summer of 1941, belonged to the Stab I./JG 54 and shows the unit badge on the nose. The 'Green Heart' Geschwader badge normally carried by Bf 109s of this unit appears to have been omitted.

**Stab I./JG 54 'Grünherz' badge**

**3./JG 54 badge**

*TOP RIGHT*: This Bf 109 F, 'Yellow 1' of 3./JG 54, was flown by Oblt. Hans Schmoller-Haldy. The Staffel badge appears on the nose and the 'Mickey Mouse' emblem positioned near the fuselage number relates to the pilot's service with 3./J88 in Spain. As the Russian campaign wore on, such emblems slowly became rarer as did personal emblems. These examples, from earlier in the war, show (*RIGHT CENTRE*) the lamb emblem of Uffz. Hemmerling of II./JG 52, who was killed on 29 July 1940, and Josef Fözo's 'Mickey Mouse' (*BELOW LEFT*), also in 1940. The identity of the pilot who flew this aircraft (*BELOW RIGHT*) marked with a hand giving the thumbs down sign, or the unit to which he belonged, is not known.